Zarathushtra and the Inmates of Paradise

Murzban Jal

AAKAR

Zarathushtra and the Inmates of Paradise
Murzban Jal

First Published 2018

ISBN 978-93-5002-581-9

Published by
AAKAR BOOKS
28 E Pocket IV, Mayur Vihar Phase I
Delhi 110 091 India
aakarbooks@gmail.com

Laser Typeset at
Sakshi Computers, Delhi

Printed at
Sapra Brothers, Noida

Rivers of wine flow in heaven,
Yes, heaven is tavern for us,
Beautiful people wait at the gates of heaven,
Yes, heaven is lustful passion for us.

Contents

Acknowledgements: Seeking Paradise

Fear and destructiveness are the major emotional sources of fascism, eros belongs mainly to democracy.

Theodor Adorno

This work is on the humanist and world historical understanding of Zoroastrianism. It is thus about ethics and good thinking. Undoubtedly ethics and good thinking necessarily lead to the projects of the Enlightenment and humanism which involve a radical transformation of the world. Paradise stands central to this imagination. Yet Paradise is a paradox. Here it is necessary to recall Omar Khayyam:

> Some of the Glories of This World; and some
> Sigh for the Prophet's Paradise to come;
> Ah, take the Cash, and let the credit go,
> Nor heed the rumble of a distant Drum.[1]

What is Paradise and who are the inmates of Paradise? This is the central question of this work. But this question boils down to the singularly important question: "What is humanity and where are we heading?" Probably no thinker other than Khayyam could address this important question. Consider this verse:

> A Book of Verses underneath the Bough,
> A Jug of Wine, a Loaf of Bread—and Thou
> Beside me singing in the Wilderness—
> Oh, Wilderness were Paradise enow![2]

While at the Centre for the Studies in Civilizations, New Delhi, when I was working on the Project of History of Indian Science, Philosophy and Culture, I took out a volume titled: *Zoroastrianism: from Antiquity to the Modern Period*. In this age of late imperialism in permanent crisis when all human creations have been turned into lethal commodities that are devouring humanity and when religion is being realized as a nuclear warhead, it is necessary to look into the actual history of religions and to rescue religion from not only the religious fundamentalists, but primarily from late imperialism which is determined to prove the existence of hell.

Kulturkritik findet sich der letzten Stufe der Dialektik von Kultur und Barbarei gegenüber: nach Auschwitz ein Gedicht zu schreiben, ist barbarisch, und das frißt auch die Erkenntnis an, die ausspricht, warum es unmöglich ward, heute Gedichte zu schreiben or "Can poetry be possible after Auschwitz?" was a question asked by Theodor Adorno.[3] Likewise Adorno had also said that "when I made my theoretical model, I could not have guessed that people would try to realize it with Molotov cocktails."[4]

One can now consequently ask: "Can one philosophize in the era of nuclear theology or theology in the age of nuclear warheads?" One can also ask: "Did Zarathushtra blunder when he invented the ideas of God and heaven and hell? Did he not know that religion would be converted not merely to Molotov cocktails, but basically to nuclear weapons? Did he not know that hell would be realized on earth itself?" And finally: "Can one really rescue religion from the religious fundamentalists?"

It is in this setting that I decided to convert my introduction to a wider public. Now at the Centre for Educational Studies, Indian Institute of Education, Pune, the legendary institute created by J.P. Naik, I have brought in this theme of philosophizing on religions in the age of the nuclear holocaust. And just as in ancient Persian theology when Ahriman, the devil, attacks the earth, the various devils in the form of educational holocaust-makers attacked this great institute. But just as in ancient Persian philosophy, the devilish attack of Ahriman on the good earth was repelled by the forces of goodness, so too at the Indian Institute of Education the repulsion of the educational devils has begun.

Besides thanking everyone at the Indian Institute of Education who thwarted the attack of the Indian Ahriman, I would also like to thank the Indian Council of Social Science Research (ICSSR), New Delhi. One has necessarily to thank Bhuvan Chandel as a source of inspiration for carrying out serious research in the social sciences. My special thanks to Jyoti Bawane, Deepak Gaikwad and Vasant Bhosle as the people who thwarted the attack of the educational holocaust-makers. Likewise one has to thank Satyabhama Kharat who agreed passionately with the basic features of Persian philosophy stating that evil exists only to be destroyed.

This little book while concentrating on Zarathushtra's impact on world history is also on the understanding of evil and its necessary destruction. This destruction needs ethics. Ethics, as Alan Badiou once said, is "the search for a good 'way of being', for a wise course of action."[5] While Badiou situated the Stoics as "the most dedicated of those who made ethics not only part of philosophical wisdom but its very core,"[6] he was caught in the Eurocentric trap, in the sense that he did not see that well beyond the horizons of Greek thinking, the ideas of evil, along with wisdom and action was conceptualized as rigorous philosophical thinking. The land was Persia and the philosopher was Zarathushtra. Badiou's "good 'way of being', for a wise course of action" is actually a Zoroastrian precept at its very core.

NOTES

1. Omar Khayyam, *Rubaiyat*, trans. Edward Fitzgerald (Tehran: Ketabsaraye, 2008), XIII.
2. Ibid., XII.
3. Theodor Adorno, 'Cultural Criticism and Society', in *Prisms*, trans. Samuel and Shirley Weber (Cambridge: The MIT Press, 1981), p. 34.
4. Quoted in Martin Jay, *The Dialectical Imagination : A History of the Frankfurt School and the Institute of Social Research 1923-1950* (Boston: Little, Brown and Company, 1973), p. 279.
5. Alan Badiou, *Ethics. An Essay on the Understanding of Evil*, trans. Peter Hallward (London: Verso, 2001), p. 1.
6. Ibid.

Prelude

He who has become wise from old origins, behold, he will at last search for the source of the future and for new origins.

Friedrich Nietzsche

Any attempt to change the world must be nourished by the image of the enslaved ancestors rather than that of liberated grandchildren.

Walter Benjamin

At present, Parsis need to be rescued from themselves.

Anahita Mukherji

To Be Wise From Old Origins

Anahita Mukherji may not get the attention that Friedrich Nietzsche or Walter Benjamin got. But her observation that the Parsis need to be rescued from themselves deserves attention. Probably the same could be said of the Iranian nation itself. Not only do the Parsis need to be rescued from themselves, but also Iran (their original homeland) needs to be rescued from itself! This seems ironical when imperialism threatens to devour Iran. What then is this irony and how can one understand it?

One begins thus this little work not only with what Friedrich Nietzsche said in *Thus Spoke Zarathustra* or what Walter Benjamin said in the *Theses on the Philosophy of History*. We begin with the first of the ironies that haunt the history of religious communities. This irony claims that it was

Zarathushtra who literally "invented" the idea of spiral history, of history that marches forward and resolves its contradictions in a Utopian future. Here he appears as an ancient dialectical materialist, or if not a dialectical materialist, then at least as a Hegelian. In this sense he has nothing in common with the quote by Benjamin and the lamentation of enslaved ancestors. It was Zarathushtra who had said that there were no enslaved ancestors and thus there was no looking backwards. Yet a sort of an irony haunts his followers.

We record it with the second of Benjamin's observations on the human condition. Note what Benjamin says:

> A Klee painting named 'Angelus Novus' shows an angel looking as though he is about to move away from something he is fixedly contemplating. His eyes are staring, his mouth is open, his wings are spread. This is how one pictures the angel of history. His face is turned toward the past. Where we perceive a chain of events, he sees one single catastrophe which keeps piling wreckage and hurls it in front of his feet. The angel would like to stay, awaken the dead, and make whole what has been smashed. But a storm is blowing in from Paradise; it has got caught in his wings with such a violence that the angel can no longer close them. The storm irresistibly propels him into the future to which his back is turned, while the pile of debris before him grows skyward. This storm is what we call progress.[1]

When dealing with the Parsis (the descendants of the Persians who are said to have fled Iran in the aftermath of the collapse of the last Persian Empire, who profess the faith of their prophet Zarathushtra), it is more of the Hegelian idea of history, of history moving forwards, recalling the Hegelian dictum: "There is no going back in history." History always marches forwards. Benjamin's angel of history seems to be totally alien to them. Yet it ought to be this very picture of the angel of history as depicted in Klee's painting that depicts the condition of these descendants of the Persians. After all, it is these very people who lose their homeland and language along with their entire culture and civilization.

Yet for them it is the future which gives them hope. The Enlightenment idea of history as eternal progress is an essential part of their repertoire. But when history ceases to march on, when history not only hops on one foot but starts marching backwards, it gets shrouded in mystery. And when this happens mythology marches onto the scene of world history. Mythology in the age of late imperialism would become not only a regression of critical thinking, it becomes fundamentalist ideology.

This present text is contextualized in the fuzzy spaces of history shrouded in myth, where the age of reason is destroyed by fundamentalisms of various sorts, most notably religious fundamentalism predicated on political theology and late imperialism in permanent crisis. And since religion in contemporary times, almost invariably brings in the question of Islamophobia, one being conscious of the same, argues out for a critical exposition of Zoroastrianism, arguing out what one calls after the twentieth century Italian Marxist, Gramsci, a "historicist and humanist" understanding of human existence and the history of human cultures and civilizations.

How does this humanization operate? It operates when one views real history, the history of humanity not burdened by ideologies. For instance, no people could be as far apart as the Zoroastrians from the Hindus. The former curse the *devas* (for the Hindus the *devas* are gods) and celebrate Ahura Mazda (the *ahuras* or the *asuras* are demons for the Hindus). Even though these two people have distinctly opposite religious-ideologies, they have met, stayed together and the Zoroastrians have blended in what would have been for them at first sight an extremely strange place. In his *Philosophy of History*, Hegel says that in Persia one:

> ......meets with European dispositions, human virtues and human passions—as soon as he crosses the Indus (i.e. the latter region), he encounters the most repellent characteristics, pervading every single feature of society.[2]

While we could critique Hegel as being a Eurocentric thinker—the way Edward Said did in his *Orientalism*—there seems to be great truth in his statement. Is this an irony once again? A rational answer is to look into history itself and see that there is ample evidence right from Darius's inscriptions to the evidence in the *Avesta* and up to Sasanian times that not merely was polytheism offensive to the Zoroastrians, but precisely the religious-ideology of their onetime brethren, was akin to demon worship. If anyone in antiquity was against what one calls "Hinduism" then it would be Zarathushtra and his Iranian followers. Buddha and B.R. Ambedkar would come later following a not altogether different path from the Persian prophet.

Hegel says that India is a "fairy region" and an "enchanted world"[3]. Hegel seems to be charitable. For the Persians (at least prior to their migration to India) would not even grant them this place of fairies and enchantment. Sociologically what is interesting is that two people with diametric opposite world-views are able to live without conflict.

Myth, History and Islamophobia

It is necessary to write the actual history of the rise and downfall of civilizations. It was Abd al-Rahman ibn Muhammed Ibn Khaldun (1332-1406), the great West Asian scholar who chalked out his theory of the rise and downfall of dynasties based on what he called *"asabiyya"* or tribal solidarity. Allen Fromherz in his *Ibn Khaldun: Life and Times*[4] talks of Ibn Khaldun on January 10, 1401 standing in front of the Mongol conqueror Timur at the gates of Damascus whereby he got inspiration for his theory of tribal solidarity and the rise and downfall of dynasties. It is this very idea that can explain the downfall of the last Persian Empire, the Sasanians, and the retreat of Zoroastrianism from the scene of world history.

According to this theory when there is lack of group feeling and shared kinship, dynasties fall. One could advance this theory and move into post-1917 history of Russia and see how the lack of group-feeling in the leadership of the Bolsheviks led to the ideological and political breakdown of solidarity between Leon Trotsky, Grigory Zinoviev, Lev Kamenev and

Nicolai Bukharin which led eventually to their murders by Stalin and the takeover of the Bolshevik Party by Stalin who appears in modern history as the classical Oriental despot.

Consequently it is necessary to view the history of the advent of the Parsis in India according to this theory. The attack of the Arabs and the advent of Islam in Iran are seen also in this perspective, besides the idea of the messianic hero which has been central to Iranian imagination. One must note that while the eternal return of the messiah was part of Zoroastrian eschatology, the Sasanian monarchy suppressed this idea. The murders of Mani (274 C.E.) and Mazdak (528 C.E.) by the Sasanian monarchy are part of this narrative of the massacre of the messianic heroes.

It is thus that we must note that Zoroastrianism did not fade away because of Islam, but because the Zoroastrianism of the Sasanian state (or Zoroastrianism "from above") did not allow subaltern Zoroastrianism, or Zoroastrianism "from below." This part of the history of Zoroastrianism and the advent of Parsis in India has to be noted. It must also be noted that Islamophobia is completely alien to the Parsis. Probably the three fundamentals of their faith: good thoughts, good words, good deeds do not allow them to be involved in hatred.

The "actual" history of the Zoroastrians arriving in India is based on a late sixteenth century document, the famous *Kisseh-e-Sanjan* or *Qesse-ye-Sanjan* ("The Story of Sanjan") composed by a certain Bahman Kaikobad (or Bahman Kay Kobād). Said to be "a Zoroastrian text written in classical metre of Persian literature" of *masnavi* variety, its aim was "to articulate a collective memory of survival and evolution in a memorable poem."[5]

The exact date of the arrival of the Zoroastrian Persians in India is never scientifically proved. Some say it is 716 C.E. while others say it is 936 C.E. This ambivalent dating is ironic, for as Hegel says that "the Persians are the first Historical People."[6] For one, this document (*Qesse-ye-Sanjan*) is of very late dating (1599 C.E.)[7], literally nine hundred years after the collapse of the Sasanian Empire in 651 C.E. While scholars have stated that this text can at best be of "folk chronology" or "questionable pseudo-history framed in doggerel", historians like Alan Williams disagree.[8] So when did the Zoroastrians come to India? Jamsheed Choksy says that the "Zoroastrian presence on the Indian subcontinent.....predate the landing of Persians at Sanjan in Gujarat, which is described in the *Qesse-ye-Sanjan* or Story of Sanjan."[9] Then why does the *Qesse-ye-Sanjan* mention an apocalypse where "more Muslim oppression" forced the Persians "to leave Iran and (thereby) they sailed to India"?[10] Was the fall of the last Persian Empire indeed apocalyptic? And would the Persians sailing to India be able to redeem the tragic fall of the Persian Empire? Williams says:

> The key to understanding of the apparent ahistoricity and inexactitude of the text is to see its fundamentally religious-mythological conception and design: it is concerned with larger themes than the syntagmatic chain of the narrative of events of this world.[11]

What then are these "larger issues" and what is the "religious-mythological conception and design" that Williams talks of? And how does one read this "design" in the age of late imperialism when its crisis is mobilizing the reactionary forces of Islamophobia? Would Zoroastrianism be mobilized by this imperialist phobia-machine especially when there is a legitimation crisis in the Islamic Republic of Iran?

Thus: "Is there a latent anti-Islamic rendering to this poem?" Consider Williams: "in the fierce clashes in battle, as allies of the indigenous Hindu forces against invading Muslims led by a certain Mahmud Shah, the Persians are said to have given their lives for India, mixing their blood with the Indian earth."[12] Consider this verse:

> You'd say that all the world was smeared with pitch,
> All struck with arrows glistening like diamonds.
> And out of all the mace-bearers and spearsmen,
> In all their thousands few remained alive.
> The land and the sky turned deepest red and black,
> The earth was tulip-red with soldiers' blood.[13]

On the one hand, this verse of the battle in Gujarat is to arouse the memory of the battles of Qadisiyya in 636 C.E. and Nehavand in 641 C.E. when the Persians fought the Arabs. On the other hand, what one gets in this verse depicting the Persians spilling their blood for the "Hindus" in battle against "Muslims" is the ideological rationale for the necessity of Parsi presence in India.

It must be noted that there is nothing called "Hinduism" (in the modern sense of the term, especially in the sense of the "Hindu"/"Muslim" conflict), and that the entire repertoire of "Hinduism" (as we know it) is a colonial construction where the Orientalists following Max Müller defined this modern myth of "Hindus" and "Hinduism", followed by the Indian upper caste elites. When we are talking of "Hindus" and "Hinduism", we are talking in a much larger historicist and humanist sense. In *Why We Are Not Hindus* we had noted the following:

> At the outset it must be said that the word "Hindu" is not something indigenous to India. It is in fact a Persian term. .... It must be understood that the original term is Persian. The Achaemenians (who ruled Iran from 559 B.C.E. to 330 B.C.E.) mention the people on the east of the river Sind as Hindus, whilst the Holy Book of the ancient Iranians—the *Avesta*—calls this land *Hapt-Hindûkn*[14]. The term in antiquity was geo-cultural and strictly from an Iranian point of view. The "Hindus" were what the Iranians called the people living on the eastern part of Sindh region. Later the Arabs too used this Persian term. Remember that for the Arabs, India was and yet is what they call "al-Hind". This geo-cultural West Asian usage was then inserted in the readings of India, especially by Albêrûnî. Mughal rule in India continued this Persian usage, but they Indianized it. What the Persians called *Hapt-Hindûkân* became "Hindustan". In ancient India, there were no people called the "Hindus". Instead one had the "*bamanshramanan*" (the Brahmans) and the "*shramanas*" (the Buddhists and the Jains). Origins of terms are many a times problematic. Whilst one can say that this is for the term "Hindu", one can also mention the paradox of the origins of other terms. For instance, Babur the founder of what we now know as the "Mughal Dynasty," disliked the term "Mughal"—Mughal is

actually the Persianized term for "Mongol". Though Babur's mother was a Chaghtai Mughal and was also the descendant of Chingiz Khan (1162-1227 C.E.)—of the pre-Islamic Tengri Shaman cult—for him, "mischief and devastation must always be expected from the Mughal horde."[15]

It is thus that we read the traditional renderings of the advent of the Persians in India. Williams talks of the "imminent arrival of hostile Muslim armies of King Mahmud Shah" that fight the "Hindu ruler."[16] Keeping this "hostile Muslim armies" and the "Hindu ruler" in brackets (to borrow a term of Edmund Husserl) along with a form of concrete historical reasoning combined with revolutionary cynicism which claims that nothing called "Hinduism" ever existed, we move into the reading of pre-capitalist communities in India and the migrant Persian recording in the *Qesse-ye-Sanjan*. It is through this concrete historical reasoning and revolutionary cynicism that we read the rationale for the presence of the Persians in India which is presented through:

1. The libation of Persian blood on Indian earth and the consequent evolution of the Iranian warrior class into mercantile class, and
2. Through artisan and mercantile settlements and activities,
3. The symbolic enthronement of the Irān Shāh *āteshbahrām* (the Zoroastrian Fire Temple where the Irān Shāh as the Holy Fire is symbolized as the New Iranian Monarch).[17]

What the first two points signify is that the class of warriors will protect India and the class of entrepreneurs will develop India, while the third point implies that the Iranian King Yazdegaard III killed in 651 C.E. is not dead. Yes, true, he is murdered in 651 C.E., but he appears in India as the Holy Fire. There is a metamorphosis at work here—the king is dead (killed in Iran) only to be reborn in India (as the Holy Fire). This metamorphosized Iranian king (as Fire) will protect India from invaders. The Parsis will be both warriors and entrepreneurs. They will both protect and develop India. The seal of patriotism is stamped on the breast of the Parsis.

So how does one read the *Qesse-ye-Sanjan*—as that of authentic history or mere fable? Further if one takes the arrival of the Zoroastrians in India only after the collapse of the Sasanians (or after the arrival of Islam) this means that no Zoroastrian lived in the Indian subcontinent and/or Zoroastrianism had no impact on Iran's then immediate neighbour and/or people of Iran and India did not meet one another. Here one needs to recall Irfan Habib's term "shared heritage" in the growth of civilizations in India and Iran.[18] In this context one must note the presence of Zoroastrians in Sri Lanka even in the times of Darius I (i.e. at the time of the Achaemenians, 550 B.C.E.–330 B.C.E.).[19] Likewise the straight-jacketing of civilizations is wrong. For instance Choksy notes of a "Maga Brahmana" a "magian (Zoroastrian) priest",[20] where this Brahman-Zoroastrian priest advised Kasyapa I (who ruled Sri Lanka from 473-91 C.E.) "to adopt the Iranian Zoroastrian practice of internment in a rock tomb 'like the corpses of the ancient Persian kings'".[21]

What happens in this space of separating Indian and Iranian histories is that this shared heritage, this shared history is completely erased. It is said that the "Parsis today have a vague idea of their history, almost all of which is an oral tradition, frequently distorted in the telling".[22] This also means that a lot of history of the Iranians in India immortalized by Firdausi in the *Sháhnáma* ("The Book of Kings") like the legendary love story of Bahram V (420–439 C.E.) nicknamed "Gur", with the daughter of Basudev, the king of Kanaui is fiction created by Firdausi (which is apparently not the case).

It must be noted, contra the theoreticians of the "clash of civilizations", that Firdausi's *Sháhnáma* is an exemplary work in Persian epic poetry, besides in Persian nationalism and to also use contemporary language "Asian multiculturalism". When asked to compose a work on the royal courts by Mahmud of Ghazni, Firdausi (a Persian Shiite) brought out an explicitly Iranian-Zoroastrian work which narrates the legendary history of Iran from Gayômart (the Iranian Adam, Gayomart, literally "the first mortal") to the last of the Sasanian kings. The fact that this is a Zoroastrian work composed by a devout Shiite has to be pointed out as also the fact that the *Shâhnâma* is also the national book of all Iranian people. It is also the "National Book" of the Zoroastrians all over the world. Not many people have thought that the Parsis—the exemplary nationalist Indians—have a foreign national book.

Unfortunately neither is the history of the Parsis, nor the culture of these Persians documented from the times of their arrival to the advent of the British. Instead of the history of the Parsi people, we have the history of the religion, the schisms in the Parsi theology and rituals in India, etc. The Parsi people are largely left out from these narratives.

The legendary Jivanji Modi had written on various aspects (religious, sociological, anthropological) of the Parsis. There are yet areas that the Parsis are well aware (which includes their songs, jokes and other types of oral histories) but not documented. The tragedy for the Parsis is that their histories are written by European and American scholars. In this sense they become the subalterns who cannot speak. Either there is a Mary Boyce, a John Hinnells, a Albert de Jong, or a Philip Kreyenbroek writing their histories. Despite the great scholarship of these Western scholars, serious ethnographical details and philosophical reflections are missed out, not to forget the latent Islamophobia of these eminent scholars. That there is much more to the Parsis than the Orientalist spectre of Islam is not known to the outside world.

But it must also be said that the flourishing of Zoroastrian Studies in Europe and the USA is also because the Indian education system after independence was caught in the feudal trap where education was (and is yet) governed not by the quest for knowledge, but governed by Caste Oligarchs who want to promote educational backwardness.

There has thus been a substantial amount of scientific research on Zoroastrianism in Europe and the USA. Yet, one can also question the authenticity of the sources of these great scholars. For example, John R. Hinnells and Alan Williams say that "though they have been in India for over 1,200 years, Parsi Zoroastrians still regard themselves as long-term émigrés from Iran, which remains their spiritual home."[23] One could ask them: "From whom did they get this information? And if indeed Iran is their "spiritual home" then why do they not protest against the mullahs and the imperialist ravaging of their "spiritual home"? Why do they not wage a war against the fascist Islamic State which is massacring the Kurds? After all, are not the Kurds their "spiritual brethren"?"

What many of these great scholars did was they secularized the methodology of Max Müller in that his method of idealistic textuality was used, but with social references. The problem is with these social references. How authentic could they be? Williams pays tribute to Shehnaz Munshi whom he calls a "true Zoroastrian" and dedicates his *The Zoroastrian Myth of Migration from Iran and Settlement in Indian Diaspora* to her[24]. What this means is that there is also a "false Zoroastrian". Who then is this "false Zoroastrian"? Further Williams also says:

> I was fortunate enough to be able to benefit from the deep learning of two High Priests, namely Dasturji Dr. Firoze M. Kotwal and Dasturji Dr. Kaikhusroo M. Jamsp Asa to whom I owe a debt of gratitude".[25]

Like Müller, Williams refers to idealistic textual scholarship, scholarship (like a lot of idealist scholarship) that is alienated from social reality. Williams also refers to Khojeste Mistree and Firoza Punthakey Mistree.[26] That all the four scholars mentioned are elites has to be mentioned. The fact that this elite scholarship is in the service of colonial academics has also to be stressed. After all, why do all these scholars interpret Zoroastrianism in the orthodox way, orthodoxy that stresses transcendental theology, endogamy and the construction of a "mythical pure Aryan community"? Is this "mythical pure Aryan community" not in the service of imperialism? Then is not Zoroastrian scholarship in creating this mythical community also creating an imperialist and almost proto-fascist theory? Is this not the "imperialism of categories" (that Ashis Nandy critiqued[27]) which is nothing but colonial scholarship? How then do we free ourselves from this ideological colonialism and the captive mind?

It is true that Zoroastrian scholarship has flourished globally. Its importance can be situated in the two stated facts:

1. The crisis of not only political Islam in Iran, but of Islam itself. This fact has hardly been noticed. While it is true that Shiite Islam is a blend of Zoroastrianism and Islam, popular culture in Iran is up in arms against Islam per se. Many Iranians would agree with the views of Mansoor Hekmat, the communist militant and founder of the Worker-Communist Party of Iran. Consider Hekmat:

   > This (Islam) is the religion of death. In reality, all religions are such but most religions have been restrained by freethinking and freedom-loving humanity over hundreds of years. This one was never restrained or controlled. With every move, it brings abominations and misery.[28]

   And:

   > Iran, in specific, is not an Islamic society as defined by Western Orientalists, Western media or the Islamic regime in Iran. Iran is a society keen for civilization and sympathetic to 21st century Western culture. It believes in science. Two generations ago, women walked the streets without veils. Western music and films have always been a part of that culture.[29]

   The global Parsis have remained far aloof from events in Iran. For them the voice of this communist militant and other claims in Iran of "back to Zoroastrianism" are totally alien to them.

2. The Parsis never wanted the question of Zoroastrianism to be akin to the "Jewish Question". The hand of history, both pre-capitalist and capitalist, in the formation of the "Jewish Question" is completely absent with the Parsis. The Parsis never wanted their existence to be reduced to that of a persecuted people. Despite the *Qessa-ye-Sanjan* never did they critique Islam or the Arab invasion in Iran. It must also be noted that the ninth century C.E. Persian book the *Bundahišn* promises the complete destruction of Arab rule from Iran[30]. Yet never

do the Parsis seek a Zoroastrian Jerusalem. In fact it is the modern Iranians who critique both Islam and the coming of the Arab religion to Iran. These details have not been highlighted. R. Cohen in his *Global Diasporas* calls the Parsis not a "travelling nation", but a "travelling religion".[31] One must stress the view of scholars like Safran who state there is "no myth of return to their original homeland."[32] Yet it must be noted that with late imperialism in permanent crisis which is furthering the crisis of the Shiite Islamic State in Iran, the question of the "return of Zoroastrianism" to Iran cannot be altogether discounted. This version forgets that the Persian Renaissance in contemporary Iran begins not with the "mythical return" of Zoroastrianism, but with Hassan Mortazavi's translation of Marx's *Capital*, Vol. I. But what will happen if Zarathushtra returns to Iran not with the *Avesta*, but with *Capital*? Will Marx become the third prophet after Zarathushtra and Muhammad?

There are even more important questions that emerge. For instance it has not been asked: "What are the noticeable parallels between not only Zarathushtra and Hegel, but primarily Zoroastrianism and Marxism?" Look at the three Zoroastrian stages:

1. *Bundahišn* (creation or before good and evil),
2. *Gumēzishn* (mixture of good and evil with the attack of Ahriman of earth) and
3. *Wizārishm* (the triumph of good over evil and the heralding of *Frašō-kereti* ("restoration", "renovation" or simply "making wonderful", in other words, "Paradise").

Now look at the three stages of Marxism:

1. Primitive communism or the absence of private property,
2. The great class societies—Asiatic mode of production, ancient, feudal and capitalist, governed by the conflict between the warring classes[33]—thus class struggle as the motor force of this stage of history, and

3. Communism with the death of private property and class struggle.

Are these not similar? Was Zarathushtra the communist of antiquity, just as Marx is the communist of the modern period?

Parsi Ethics, Antiquity and the Spirit of Modernity

Though the history of Zoroastrianism spans from the ancient Indo-Iranian world to modern times, it is modernity, especially the rise of industrial capitalism, which would interest the critical reader. Yet it must be noted that modernity, even in Western Europe, did not develop from its own cranium. As Jürgen Habermas says:

> The expression 'modernity' refers back to the past of classical antiquity precisely in order to comprehend itself as the result of a transition from the old to the new.[34]

Though modernity is "consciousness of a new era developed,"[35] this is "through a renewed relationship to classical antiquity."[36] Consequently "the classical world was regarded as the normative model to be imitated."[37]

Consequently the dialogue between Persian antiquity and Parsi modernity in central to this little book *Zarathushtra and the Inmates of Paradise* which is also a philosophical and historical reading of Zoroastrianism from the teachings of the prophet Zarathushtra to the modern Parsis. It narrates the history of Zoroastrianism keeping in mind what the German philosopher G.W.F. Hegel had called "the cunning of reason" (*die List der Vernunft*) and what Marxism has called "unintended consequences of history", where Zoroastrianism as probably one of the great influences on world history (till some time in the middle of the seventh century C.E.) literally regressed from the stage of history. In this narrative of *ironical history,* not only are the teachings of Zoroastrianism taken into consideration, along with their impact on Judaism, Christianity and Islam, but one also discusses Nietzsche who immortalized Zarathushtra in his *Thus Spoke Zarathustra.* This book also takes into consideration the irony of how both political theologies in general and the ideology of the contemporary Islamic Republic of Iran owes its political theory neither to Christianity nor to Islam, but to a Sasanian Zoroastrian document known as the *Letter of Tansar*. Is this not the cunning of reason? For how can the ideological grounding of the Islamic Republic of Iran be based on an ancient Zoroastrian state document? To understand this, one needs to go into the interiors of history.

Zoroastrianism has its rigorous history, including its own mythological history from the "first human" and the "first male and female"—the ancient Persian Adam and Eve. For certain reasons, this mythological history is totally forgotten by the modern Parsis. If this mythological history appears, it appears in the eleventh century poet Firdausi's masterpiece *Sháhnáma*. Ironically the modern Parsis are totally oblivious of this Iranian past. They are oblivious of the legends of the Iranian nation. It is in fact the contemporary Iranians who have the historical memory of the Iranian nation. For the Parsis, to recall Habermas once again, there is:

> ...a radicalized consciousness of modernity that detached itself from all previous historical connection and understood itself in abstract opposition to tradition and history as a whole.[38]

And:

> What was considered modern was what assisted the spontaneously self-renewing historical contemporaneity of the *Zeitgeist* to find its objective expression. The characteristic feature of such works is the moment of novelty, the New, which will itself be surpassed and devalued in turn by the innovations of the next style.[39]

What the modern Parsis did was they almost altogether detached themselves from their language, despite strongly being ideologically and culturally rooted in the Persian ethos. The idea of the "new" was also central to their imagination, along with the question of what one calls "benevolence".[40] It is thus that quite often, the history of the modern Zoroastrians in India is depicted as the history of an elite, in fact as a colonial elite. There is no major narrative of the poor Parsis. This means that the Parsis are some sort of Utopian Socialists who created their form of classless society devoid of poverty well before Karl Marx came onto the scene of history. T.M. Luhrmann's classic, *The Good Parsi: The Fate of a Colonial Elite in a Postcolonial Society*[41] is an example of this sort of Western cultural anthropological rendering. There are also other renderings that appeared in the pages of the *Economic & Political Weekly* where the Parsis appear as a comprador class. Amalendu Guha, for instance, classifies the early Parsi bourgeoisie as comprador.[42] While Guha, unlike Luhrmann worked with statistical data, bringing in also the question of caste in India and the absence of caste in the Parsis that enabled them to rise as a bourgeois class, the mechanisms of the rise of the Parsis from a migrant agricultural-based community to global entrepreneurs was never explored.

The problem is situated in a form of nationalist historiography which did not spare even the Indian Marxists. While E.M.S. Namboodiripad and following him Prabhat Patnaik situated the problem of Indian stagnation in the Brahmanical counterrevolution against Buddhism where productive labour was relegated as "unclean" and "impure",[43] Irfan Habib situates Indian "backwardness" only with the coming of the British. According to Habib there were "potentialities of development in the Indian economy prior to the British conquest."[44] This means there were distinct potentialities of *capitalist development* before the advent of colonialism in India.

While Habib's argument of the possible growth of capitalism in Mughal India cannot be dismissed, one forgets that caste led to stagnancy and how in the Indian variant of the Asiatic mode of production of village communities based on the caste system of social exclusion, not only was free labour excluded, but due to the classification of the artisans as the unclean untouchables (at least since Adi Shankara's counterrevolution); the development of industrial capital was precluded. India could develop merchant's capital and usurer's capital, but not industrial capital; just as under the hegemony of the Brahman, India could develop its so-called "spiritual" philosophies, but not its indigenous sciences. What Western modernity did was on the one hand to enter India under the economic logic of colonialism, and on the other hand, to let the project of modernity take a course where it was used to destabilize colonial rule. One recalls Marx's double role of colonialism in his *The British Rule in India*, destructive and regenerative. It destroyed the village communities, and in doing so, was supposed to destroy the caste system.

That the Parsis could embrace modernity was on the one hand, the continuation of the Persian love for the "new" and the "unknown". But it was also the case that the Parsis have been comfortable with cultures linked with developed forces of production. The political economy of backwardness and scarcity has always been an unpleasant experience for them. This dialectic of modernity then propelled them to a contradictory position: on the one hand, they became "elites"; and on the other hand, they also became a part of the subaltern vanguard in the struggle against colonialism. Dadabhai Naoroji, Dinshaw Wacha, Pherozeshah Mehta, Behram Malbari and Shapurji Saklatvala are the figures who form the vanguard against feudalism, capitalism and colonialism. Shapurji Saklatvala (1874-1936), one must note, though coming from the House of the Tatas (his mother was the sister of J.N. Tata (1830-1904), thereby making him an uncle of the legendary capitalist J.R.D. Tata (1904-1993), was a communist and one of the early members of the Communist Party of Great Britain, besides being thrice Member of Parliament (UK) twice as a socialist and once as a communist. Is this one more of the ironies of history with references to the Parsis?

Yes it is true, for the Parsis from time immemorial, the question for the "new" has been central to their culture. Yes it is also true that "backwardness" is something that they have always abhorred. But if indeed the Parsis were always uncomfortable with the political economy and culture of "backwardness", then why did they sail to India, the alleged land of caste stratification and economic backwardness? It has thus been asked as to "why a group of Persian migrants would have chosen to settle here than elsewhere."[45] Consider Hegel's observation:

> While China and India remain stationary, and perpetuate a natural vegetative existence even to the present time, this land (Persia) has been subject to those developments and revolutions, which alone manifest a historical condition.[46]

Then why did the Persians with their culture of "development" and "revolutions" flee to India? Was this not a part of the cunning of reason? Keeping this aspect of the Parsis as the practitioners of development and revolutions, let us see how they not only move into the era of modernity, but become one of the harbingers of modernity.

Besides the Asiatic mode of production with caste forming with what Marx called the "solid foundation" of despotism[47], there is also the cultural part where the Parsis could become the harbingers of social democracy in South Asia. There is a logic of continuity that forms some sort of cultural background of the Zoroastrians. The idea of *payman*, or the "correct measure" stands out. And it is this Persian "correct measure" which would also lead then to be vanguards of the development of early capitalism in India.

To understand the cultural politics of this "correct measure" it is necessary to go into the legend of Jamshid, who Indian history knows as "Yama". According to Persian legend, Jamshid could flirt like Faust with Ahriman to extract this correct measure. But what impact did Jamshid's extraction of the "correct measure" have on present times? What is this "correct measure" and how is it related to capitalist development?

One needs to relate this "correct measure" with the question of the commodity principle that Marx raises in the very first pages of the first volume of *Capital*. If surplus in the sense of profit-making enterprise could be said to be the political economy of rational welfare capitalism and the equitable distribution the essence of socialism, then both the production of surplus and the rational distribution form a part of the cultural logic of the Zoroastrians. The fact that the pioneers of not only industrialism, but also the democratic movement, were Parsis ought not to be surprising.

Humanization Needed

The purpose of this short work is on the humanization of history. There is enough demonization of people, their cultures and civilizations. Enough is enough! Both the *Rg Veda* and the *Avesta* contain ample material to understand the proto-Indo-Iranian culture from whence both modern Iran and India came into being. Themes like the common abode of these two people, the shared concerns of the moral order of the universe, the stories of creation in the *Rg Veda* and the *Avesta* and the shared mythologies, while known to professional scholars, are sadly forgotten in the public space. One has forgotten Avesta as the language of the Zoroastrian Books and its comparison to Old Sanskrit. One has thus also forgotten the family resemblances between these two languages, and also forgotten the question of the "original homeland" of the Indo-Iranians (both the Avestan and the Rg Vedic people) which is traced to North Europe. While colonialism tore apart the soul of the colonized people, it made a class of native elites who would ape the colonial elites, whereby this common "natural history" of a sizeable part of the world is literally forgotten.

What one indeed needs to forget is the horrible "clash of civilizations" thesis, and to remember the story of human civilization. True there have been many imaginary happenings, but quite often these have been determined by secular and humanist worldviews that have largely governed the history of the subaltern masses of West and South Asia. One must here point out the cult that synthesized Hinduism, Zoroastrianism, Christianity and Islam (which also included Greek philosophy): the cult of Azar Kaivan. It is possible that the origins of such secular-subaltern renderings of religion of the popular classes can be located in the Azar Kayvani tradition, since the *Dabestan-e Madaheb*, a seventeenth century syncretistic book, that synthesizes Zoroastrianism, Greek, Sabean, Hinduism, Buddhism, Judaism, Christianity, Islam, besides other religious sects. It is usually said that the author is Mir Du'l-feqar Ardestani (1671–70), better known as Molla Mowbad or Mowbadshah, who belonged to a Persian Shiite family, and became a follower of the Azar Kayvani sect while still a child. As we shall see it is this non-partisan syncretized tradition that was taken by the Mughal emperor, Akbar, and institutionalized as state ideology.

Whether Ahura Mazda (the Zoroastrian understanding of God) did or did not seep into West and South Asian ideology of popular religions cannot be determined quite so easily. But due to the geo-politics of American imperialism, the name of Ahura Mazda in its Modern Persian name of Hormuz (distorted from the Middle Persian "Ohrmuzd", *meaning* Ahura Mazda), does ring out. The Strait of Hormuz has now become the flashpoint between the forces of American imperialism and the state of Iran.

In this sense, Zarathushtra was correct in claiming that the clash between the opposite forces—of light and darkness, of Ohrmuzd (Hormuz) and Ahriman, (rather: of imperialism and anti-imperialism)—has not quite ended. In this sense one wonders what Benjamin's metaphor of the angel of history looking backwards despite being blown forward can mean today. Either one inevitably has to clash with evil (to be precise with imperialism), or as Gerhard Scholem said (that Benjamin uses in his analysis of the painter Klee), one is plagued by the Hamletean, if not the Faustian situation:

My wing is ready for flight,
I would like to turn back,
If I stayed timeless time,
I would have little luck.[48]

NOTES

1. Walter Benjamin, 'Theses on the Philosophy of History', in *Illuminations*, trans. Harry Zohn (Glasgow: Fontana/Collins, 1979), p. 259.
2. G.W.F. Hegel, *The Philosophy of History*, trans. J. Sibree (New York: Prometheus Books, 1991), p. 17.
3. Ibid.
4. See Allen Fromherz in his *Ibn Khaldun. Life and Times* (Edinburgh University Press, 2010). Also see Ibn Khaldun, *The Muqaddimah, as Introduction to History*, trans. Rosenthal (London: Routledge & Kegan Paul, 1967); Leon Goldsmith, 'Syria's Alawites and the Politics of Sectarian Insecurity. A Khaldunian Perspective', in *Ortadoğu Etütleri*, Vol. 3, No. 1, July 2011.
5. Alan Williams, 'The Qessa-ye-Sanjan', John R. Hinnells and Alan Williams, (ed.), *Parsis in India and the Diaspora* (London and New York: Routledge, 2008), p. 17.
6. G.W.F. Hegel, op. cit.
7. Alan Williams, op. cit., p. 20.
8. Alan Williams, *The Zoroastrian Myth of Migration from Iran and Settlement in the Indian Diaspora. Text. Translation and Analysis of the 16th Century Qesse-ye-Sanjan* (Leiden: Brill, 2009).
9. See Jamsheed K. Choksy, 'Iranians and Indians on the Shores of Serendib (Sri Lanka)', in John R. Hinnells and Alan Williams, (ed.), *Parsis in India and the Diaspora* (London and New York: Routledge, 2008), p. 185.
10. See Alan Williams, 'The Qesse-ye-Sanjan', John R. Hinnells and Alan Williams, (ed.), *Parsis in India and the Diaspora* (London and New York: Routledge, 2008), p. 22.
11. Ibid., p. 21.
12. Ibid., pp. 18-19.
13. Quoted in Ibid., p. 19.
14. See the Zoroastrian *Pahlavi Vendidâd* (Zand=Î Jvît-Dêv=Dât), transliteration and translation by B.T. Anklesaria (Mumbai: K. R. Cama Oriental Institute, 2002), p. 12.
15. See my *Why We Are Not Hindus* (Delhi: Aakar Books, 2016), pp. 22-3. Also see Zahir Uddin Muhammad Babur's, *Babur Nama*, ed. Dilip Hiro (London: Penguin Books, 2006) on Babur's statement

of the "mischief and devastation (that) must always be expected from the Mughal horde."

16. Alan Williams, 'The Qesse-ye-Sanjan', p. 22.
17. Ibid., p. 19.
18. Irfan Habib, (ed.) *A Shared Heritage. The Growth of Civilizations in India & Iran* (New Delhi: Tulika Books, 2002).
19. See Jamsheed K. Choksy, op. cit., pp., 181-210.
20. Ibid., p. 181.
21. Ibid., p. 183-4.
22. See Rukshana Nanji and Homi Dhalla, 'The Landing of the Zoroastrians at Sanjan. The Archaeological Evidence', in John R. Hinnells and Alan Williams, (ed.), *Parsis in India and the Diaspora*, p. 35.
23. See John R. Hinnells and Alan Williams, 'Introduction' in John R. Hinnells and Alan Williams, (ed.), *Parsis in India and the Diaspora* (London and New York: Routledge, 2008), p. 2.
24. Alan Williams, *The Zoroastrian Myth of Migration from Iran and Settlement in the Indian Diaspora. Text. Translation and Analysis of the 16th Century Quesse-ye-Sanjan* (Leiden: Brill, 2009).
25. Ibid., p. XI.
26. Ibid.
27. Ashis Nandy, 'The Politics of Secularism and the Recovery of Religious Tolerance' in Rajeev Bhargava, (ed.), *Secularism and Its Critics* (Delhi: Oxford University Press: 1998), pp. 321-344.
28. *Islam and De-Islamization*, Interview of Mansoor Kekmat with Negah Publications, January 1999
29. *Islam is Part of the 'Lumpenism' in Society*, Interview of Mansoor Hekmat with Radio Hambastegi in Malmoe, Sweden. Strangely these alleged communist points of view forget completely Marx's and Engels' views on Islam. One can see Peter Hudis, 'Marx Among the Muslims', in *Capitalism, Nature, Socialism*, Vol. 15, 2004, Issue 4 for Marx's views on Islam as revolutionary ideology.
30. See *Zand-Ākāsīh. Iranian or Greater Bundahišn*, transliteration and translated by B.T. Anklesaria (Bombay: Rahnumae Mazdaysnan Sabha, 1956).
31. R. Cohen, *Global Diasporas: An Introduction* (London: Routledge , 1997), p. 188f. Also see John R. Hinnells and Alan Williams, op. cit., p. 3.

32. See W. Safran, 'Diasporas on Modern Societies: Myths of Homeland and Return', in *Diaspora*, Spring, 1991. Also see John R. Hinnells and Alan Williams, op. cit., p. 3.
33. See Karl Marx, 'Preface' to *A Contribution to the Critique of Political Economy* (Moscow: Progress Publishers, 1978), p. 22.
34. Jürgen Habermas, 'Modernity: An Unfinished Project', in Maurisio Passerin D'entreves and Seyla Benhabib, (ed.), *Habermas and the Unfinished Project of Modernity. Critical Essays on The Philosophical Discourse of Modernity* (Cambridge: Polity Press, 1996), p. 39.
35. Ibid.
36. Ibid.
37. Ibid.
38. Ibid.
39. Ibid.
40. See John R. Hinnells, 'The Flowering of Zoroastrian Benevolence', in *Papers in Honour of Mary Boyce*, ed. H.W. Bailey, A.D.H. Bivar, J. Duchesne-Guillemin and John R. Hinnells (Leiden: E.J. Brill, 1985).
41. T.M. Luhrmann, *The Good Parsi. The Fate of a Colonial Elite in a Postcolonial Society* (Delhi: Oxford University Press, 1996).
42. Amalendu Guha, 'More About the Parsis Seths. Their Roots, Entrepreneurship and Comprador Role, 1650-1918' in *Economic & Political Weekly*, Vol. 19, Issue 3, January, 21, 1984.
43. See *Prabhat Patnaik,* 'The Left in Decline', in *Economic & Political Weekly*, Vol. 47, No. 10, March 10, 2012, which has also been included in my (ed.) *Challenges for the Indian Left* (Delhi: Aakar Books, 2017), pp. 457-487.
44. Irfan Habib, 'Potentialities of Capitalistic Development in the Economy of Mughal India', in *Essays in Indian History. Towards a Marxist Perception* (New Delhi: Tulika, 1995), p. 180.
45. See Rukshana Nanji and Homi Dhalla, 'The Landing of the Zoroastrians at Sanjan. The Archaeological Evidence', in John R. Hinnells and Alan Williams, (ed.), *Parsis in India and the Diaspora*, p. 35.
46. G.W.F. Hegel, op. cit.
47. Karl Marx, 'The British Rule in India', in *Marx. Engels. On Colonialism* (Moscow: Progress Publishers, 1976), p. 40.
48. Quoted in Walter Benjamin, op. cit.

Zarathushtra and the Inmates of Paradise

There is no cultural document that is not at the same time a record of barbarism.

Walter Benjamin

The "Cunning of Reason"

The "cunning of reason" (*die List der Vernunft*) is one of Hegel's terms, not often used in the philosophy of religions and human civilizations. Nor is Benjamin's statement which says that "there is no cultural document that is not at the same time a record of barbarism"[1] a part of the general theory of religions. Yet it is through this intertwining of religion and cunningness of reason that is manifested as barbarism that opens the reading of the text *Zarathushtra and the Inmates of Paradise*.

Paradise which has been immortalized by Persian poetry, especially that of Rumi, and now a part of the war manuals of theological fundamentalists, is actually a Zoroastrian invention. The rivers of wine which seem to be part of the Koranic narrative have their roots in ancient Persia. And so does dialectics, which was made central to the philosophies of Hegel and Marx, central to Persian philosophy. Hegel in his *History of Philosophy* and *Philosophy of History* talks in detail of Zarathushtra and Persian philosophy as would Goethe in his *West-East Divan* and Nietzsche in his classic *Thus Spoke Zarathustra*.[2]

While these points refer to European reflections on this Persian sage, the importance comes up, especially in relation to the crisis of political Islam in Iran. If the Persians are indeed people with history, as Hegel suggested, then the history of pre-Islamic Iran cannot be totally forgotten. Unlike the ideology of Islamophobia, we do not intend to replace one prophet with another prophet, or one religion with another messianic religion. What has been forgotten is what Hegel calls "Universal History"[3] does not relate the histories of people in isolation from one another. Instead following the dialectical method one sees historical events in the forms of historical connectivity. Thus we view not the clash between Zoroastrianism and Islam, but the interconnectivity between the two. The clashes as we very well know, are to be understood in the site of class struggles, the political conflicts emerging thereon and the changes in religious ideologies.

Contextualizing Zoroastrianism As "Universal History"

"Light", so Hegel once said, "belongs to the World of Consciousness—to Spirit."[4] It is in this terrain of Light-Consciousness-Spirit that we begin our exposition. Zoroastrianism—or *Zarathushtri Mazdayasnean Dîn*—"Zarathushtra's path to the celebration of wisdom"—was the official religion of the ancient Iranians founded by the prophet Zarathushtra (literally "he of the Golden Light" and "the herald of the Golden Dawn"), and as the official Iranian faith lasted till the collapse of the Sasanian Empire in 651 C.E. For the Greeks and the Romans he appears as Zoroaster (*astrothutes*, "the star priest" or "the star diviner" derived from the Greek word *astron* or *aster* implying star)[5]. Zoroastrianism is the first monotheistic religion[6], accompanying Vedic religion. The irony is that the three great "Semitic" religions, Judaism, Christianity and Islam would emerge from the cranium of this non-Semitic thought and life-world.

As religion, culture and philosophy, Zoroastrianism is a bridge between the East and the West, the sister religion of early Hinduism and the religious philosophy that inspired Judaism, Christianity and Islam, besides being closely related to

Northern Buddhism. With the unification of the Iranian tribes and the formation of the Persian Empire by Cyrus the Great in the sixth century B.C.E., ancient Iran had opened two historical pathways: the Eastern pathway which linked Hinduism and Buddhism to Iran and the Western pathway which linked the Egyptians, Babylonians, Romans and Greeks directly to Iran and the Zoroastrians. Probably the least known fact is that Greek philosophy and the origins of Western civilization also lie in Iran.[7] Anaximander of Miletus (c. 610-546 B.C.E.) is the starting point in the marriage between Iranian and Greek ideas that flowered in Plato's academy and culminated in the refuge of the Greek philosophers in Sasanian Iran. This cultural traffic in the ancient world gave rise to three great civilizations: the Iranian, the Indian and the Hellenist civilizations.

After the onset of feudalism in Iran and the crisis of the breakdown of the centralized Iranian state led by the king of kings (*Shāhān Shāh-ī-Ērān*) accompanied by the fratricidal conflicts for the throne of Iran culminating in the victory of the Arabs over the Iranians in the two fateful battles in 636 C.E. (Qadisiyya) and 641 C.E. (Nehavand), the national power of the last Zoroastrian Empire—the Sasanians (220-651 C.E.)—was lost. With the loss of political power, so too was lost the influence of Zoroastrianism as the dominant power in Iran, but also in the greater part of the civilized world. Post-651 C.E. a group of Persians left their homeland and arrived at the Western coast of India. The date of the arrival of these Persians (since then known as the "Parsis") varies. Sometimes said to be in the eighth-century, sometimes in the tenth century C.E.[8]. There is also a view that well before the collapse of the Sasanians and well into the days of "glory" of the Iranian Empire, a Persian philosopher, sensing the disastrous consequences of war-torn Iran and the imperial conflicts between Rome and Iran under the monarch Khausrau II, also known as Parvez or "the Victorious" (590-628 C.E.), predicted the downfall of the Zoroastrian-Iranian power and set sail to India. Since then the story of Zoroastrianism moves from the story of "glory" to "exile", or as the celebrated Iranianist R.C. Zaehner once called it: from dawn to twilight[9]. The glory of Zoroastrianism runs from 1500 B.C.E. to 651 C.E. The most eventful epochs are in the times of the Achaemenians and the Sasanians.

The roots of Zoroastrianism lie, of course, in Iran. But the branches and the shadows fall on other parts of the world. The story begins in the period of the Indo-Iranian Great Migrations where the first single voice from this period is heard—the voice of Zarathushtra. What he leaves behind is the *Gathas* (literally "The Songs")—a collection of philosophical hymns. Since, like Hinduism, the religious works were composed in the form of mantric poetry and memorized by professional hereditary priests, the works of Zoroastrianism are alive even today some three thousand five hundred years after they were first composed. Unlike the *Rg Veda* which is a sister text comprising one thousand and twenty-eight hymns, the *Gathas* are much smaller. But if one has to believe the Greek philosopher Hermippus (third century B.C.E.) then Zarathushtra is said to have composed two million verses. What is extant today is a small compact philosophical treatise that ranges from (1) the first statement on monotheism and the harmony of the spheres, (2) the conflict of the two warring forces in nature—the active and the reactive forces—to (3) the doctrine of human freedom and (4) the metaphysics of morality: "good thoughts, good words and good deeds." Even today it is these four principles that stand in the hearts of the Zoroastrians.

The voice of Zarathushtra emerges in the Iranian Late Bronze Age. The first sound that emerges from Zarathushtra is that of laughter at the time of his birth.[10] His life that is depicted is of a young rebel in defiance with the norms of his times. The people stated to be his antagonists are the priests (*Karpans*) and the kings (*Kavis*). In the court of the ruling elite—a Persian text calls it "an assembly of wizards"[11]—his status as the exalted one is challenged. He is given some water said to be some sort of 'magical' potion to cure him of his defiance. Zarathushtra gives the water to the horses and says that it was useless going to the residence of the priests but by giving water to the horses, his soul had expanded.[12] Once more he is brought to the court of the iniquitous where a bowl of mare's milk is put before him and he is asked to consecrate it. Zarathushtra kicks the bowl and says: "I reverence righteousness. I reverence the righteous and the poor men and women."[13] For Zarathushtra, not only is righteousness kept at the central motif of his teachings, but all people irrespective of classes and nations are considered equal, especially men and women. Righteousness is, as the ninth century C.E. encyclopaedic text the *Dînkard* claims, "a thing to perform."[14]

The time and homeland of Zarathushtra is much debated, the dates ranging from 6000 B.C.E. to 258 years before Alexander, i.e. till around the sixth century B.C.E., and his birthplace ranging from Azerbaijan to Afghanistan. According to Pliny's *Natural History*:

> Without doubt magianship arose in Persia with Zoroaster. On this our authorities are agreed, but whether he was the only one of that name, or whether there was also another one afterwards, is not clear. Eudoxus [of Cnidus 408/391-355/338 B.C.E., a disciple of Plato], who wished magianship to be acknowledged as the noblest and the most useful of the schools of philosophy, declared that Zoroaster lived 6000 years before Plato's death [349/348 B.C.E.] and Aristotle [384-322 B.C.E.] agrees with him. Hermippus [III century B.C.E.], a most distinguished writer about every aspect of magianship, and an exponent of two million verses composed by Zoroaster, added summaries too to his roles, and gave Agonaces as the teacher by whom he has said that he had been instructed, assigning to the man himself a date 5000 years before the Trojan war [which was according to Greek calculations ca. 1200 B.C.E.].[15]

Diogenes Laertius held the view that :

> In his book of mathematics the Platonist Hermodorus counts 5000 years from the Magians, the first of whom according to him was Zoroaster the Persian, up to the fall of Troy; but Xanthus the Lydian counts 6000/600 years from Zoroaster to Xerxus's crossing (of the Hellespont) [480 B.C.E.].[16]

Since the *Avesta* (the Holy Book of the Zoroastrians, literally "The Foundational Text") talks of the Iranian homeland as *Airyana-Vaejah* wherein dwells ten months winter and two months summer[17], it was thought that the original homeland was in the Arctic. B.G. Tilak was of this view. There is yet no clear-cut conclusion as to why the Indo-Iranians left this land of winter. Since the *Avesta* talks of the flood and how the legendary Iranian King Yima (in Iranian folklore Yima is "the first man and first king", in India he appears as Yama, while in Middle Persian he is Jamshid) built an underground shelter (*vara*) taking with him the seeds of plants and humanity,[18] it is supposed that a natural disaster compelled them to leave *Airyana-Vaejah* and move via the South Russian Steppes and settle in the Iranian plateau sometime in the second millennium B.C.E.

The geography that Zarathushtra indicates is not harsh. Instead the picture of his homeland is pastoral. It is a pre-nomadic and pre-agricultural economy.[19] The harshness depicted in the *Gathas* is the harshness of the social and political environment probably echoing the breakdown of the Old Indo-Iranian gens. With the breakdown of the primitive communist societies, the second millennium B.C.E. witnessed the war between two classes—the pastoralists and the chariot-wielding hunters. It is probable that the chariot had become the vehicle used by the Indo-Iranians in raiding neighbouring tribes and killing both people and cattle. Zarathushtra uses two metaphors for mobilizing his people against the raiders tribes—the first is of "the soul of the cow" (*Geush Urvan*)[20], also called "the soul of the earth" which stands for some sort of a naturalism and humanism in the first possible critique of class societies. The second metaphor is of the lie (*Drujas*)[21], brought about by the violent raider communities. Zarathushtra mentions fleeing from these people not sure where to go.[22] He is only with a small band of followers who are taught by Zarathushtra to seek "the Bliss which the Beloved (*Fryō*) grants to the lover (*fryāi*)."[23] Because of Zarathushtra's statement, it is postulated that it is he who is the original Sufi, and that *Zarathushtri Mazdayasnean Dîn* as the foundation of monotheism is in actuality a humanism and a naturalism of the Sufi Order where the Bliss of Love takes centre stage. It is an Iranian 'king' Vistaspa who listens to his philosophy of the harmony of the spheres and the conflict between good and evil, converts to his religion and gives him refuge. Since then the first community of the Zoroastrian fraternity was created. Seeking Mazda, or wisdom, with the eye of the good mind (*Vohu Manah*) remains Zarathushtra's central thought. One has to seek wisdom (*Mazda*) and one also has to open one's eyes of the good mind.

It is probably one thousand years later with the foundation of the Persian Empire under Cyrus the Great, himself said to be a Zoroastrian[24], that the Magis (the followers of Zarathushtra) were able to preach without opposition. With the advent of Darius to the throne of Iran, it is certain that Zoroastrianism became the religion of the whole of Iran. Yet the Achaemenian state did not become a theological state. The Behistun inscription describes Darius's conflict with a certain "Gaumata the Magus who called himself Bardiya" who seized the throne of Iran by proclaiming to be a son of Cyrus. That there was a conflict between the pseudo-son of Cyrus (who also calls himself a Magi) indicates that there was a distinct conflict between, at least, Darius and a priest. Whether this was symptomatic of a line of demarcation drawn between the Magis and the rule of the kings in Achaemenian Iran is not known. But most certainly Darius's reference to one God: Ahura Mazda also called "the Great God" (*baga vazarka*) and one king: "the great king" (*xāsyathiya vazarka*)[25] independent of any human intermediaries makes it clear that Achaemenian Iran, which also strove for a universal world empire, did not enforce its religion on the masses. Instead it became not only an archetypal multicultural state of antiquity, but also the first probable multicultural state of the ancient world. Not only were national and linguist minorities protected by the Persian state, but the Persians also rescued those suffering from persecution by foreign governments. The Achaemenian inscriptions, both Cyrus's inscription in Babylon and Darius in Behistun, indicate that religions other than Zoroastrianism were not only allowed but also actively cultivated. The appearance of Cyrus, Darius, Xerxes and Artaxerxes in the *Bible* as the saviours of the Jews from the state sponsored persecution by the Babylonian ruling classes is testimony to the multiculturalism of the Persians. With the advent of the Achaemenians in the Iranian government not only were all Iranian-speaking people—from Media, Persia, Afghanistan, Azerbaijan, Turkmenistan, and Tajikistan to Armenia—united under one federation, but also Egypt and Babylon were under Persian rule. It is ironical that almost the same sort of 'glories' of the Iranians has been mentioned as late as 620 C.E. Within three decades of the last glories of the Zoroastrians, the last of the Zoroastrian regimes would wither away, almost never to rise ever again. Zarathushtra's original plea of having only a "small following" (*kamnā nā*)[26] would return to haunt his followers.

The history of Zoroastrianism from 1500 B.C.E. to the present has been classified in three epochs: (1) origins, (2) growth and zenith, and (3) invasion, migration and decline, while the religious ideology of Zoroastrianism is classified as (1) catholic and multicultural, and (2) dualist and orthodox. The 'Book' of Zoroastrianism is the *Avesta* ("The Foundational Text") and though originally comprised of twenty-one volumes is now extant only in five books: (1) the *Yasna* ("worship", "ceremony", "celebration") which includes Zarathushtra's *Gathas*, (2) *Visparat* ("the spiritual lords"), (3) *Vi-dēva-dāt* (later corrupted into *Vendidâd* or the "law against the demons"), (4) the *Yashts*, ("worship") and (5) *Khorde Avesta* ("the smaller *Avesta*"). As Zarathushtra's original sayings are found only in the *Gathas*, it has been debated whether the later *Avesta* is to be taken as the continuation of his teachings, or whether there is an epistemological break in the *Avesta*; and the later *Avesta* is to be understood as a part of a heterogeneous liturgical Iranian tradition, where the Magis used Zarathushtra's own name to propagate these rather heterogeneous ideas. There is no decisive conclusion to these debates and are raised repeatedly not only by Zoroastrian scholarship but also by the liberals and the orthodox Zoroastrians in contemporary debates regarding the real meaning of Zoroastrianism. Following this master-text of Zoroastrianism are also the *Zand* ("The Commentaries" or "Interpretations") and other Middle Persian or Pahlavi works composed in Sasanian times and in the early Islamic epoch.

One thus reads the Zoroastrian Book—the *Avesta*—with the sub-texts to this master book, namely the *Zand*. Along with these works are the ninth century classics of which the *Dînkard* ("Acts of Religion") and the *Bundahišn* ("Creative Evolution") stand out as monumental works on Zoroastrianism. As mentioned before, the *Avesta* was composed in the oral tradition.[27] The literal rendering starts only with the first Sasanian monarch Ardashīr Papakan (226-241 C.E.) assisted by the great Zoroastrian prelate Tansar and carried on by Ardashīr's son Shapur I (241-271 C.E.). The translations into Pahlavi or Middle Persian were carried out during the reign of Shapur II (309-379 C.E.) and completed by the third of the three great Zoroastrian prelates: Ārdubād ī Maharaspandān, with commentaries later added during the reign of Khausrau I also called "Anoshirwan" or "of the Immortal Soul" (531-579 C.E.). The three great Zoroastrian prelates: Tansar, Kirder and Ārdubād ī Maharaspandān would be the philosopher-ideologists par excellence not only in Sasanian times but also in the history of Zoroastrianism. Besides these names, the names of Ārdubād ī Zarduštān, Khausrau I, Baxt-Āfrid, Ādur-farnbag Farrokhzāndān and Ārdubād ī Ēmētān emerge as Zoroastrian philosopher-ideologists. Their contribution to the development of Zoroastrianism, especially gnomic, *andraz* literature is invaluable.

But the Book itself in its extant form, and distinct from the original composition, at least till the time of Alexander's invasion of Iran and the destruction of the *Avesta* (as also from the Sasanian rendering) exists only in fragments. Despite the fragmented condition it is larger than the Christian Gospels and the *Koran*.[28] There are now only five parts of the *Avesta* as distinct from the original twenty-one books (*Nasks*). If Ardashīr could conceive (or continue the Parthian project) of gathering the *Avesta* from all over the Iranian-speaking lands and then rework the whole, thus making possible for the Zoroastrian renaissance; then after the victory of the Arabs there was the second renaissance following the defeat of the Umayyad dynasty at the hands of the Abbasids. But with further attacks in the twelfth and thirteenth centuries in Iran by the Turks and the Mongols, as well as the hegemony of Islam as the new messianic religious-ideology of Iran, any further renaissance of Zoroastrianism was impossible. The conditions of the Zoroastrians after the downfall of the Sasanians has much been debated with the conclusion that "much slaughter and a number of enforced conversions" was carried out.[29]

The *Avesta*, the *Zand* and *Pazand* along with the Pahlavi works are the main sources for the understanding of Zoroastrianism. But besides these works, one also has the Iranian inscriptions that the Achaemenians, Parthians, and the Sasanians left behind on their great monuments, along with coins, pottery and other artefacts. Besides archaeological evidence of Zoroastrianism in the heartland of the Persian Empire, there are also ample evidences of Zoroastrian ossuaries, paintings, sculptures, etc., in Central Asia where the Iranian tribes (the Bactrians, Sogdians, Sakas and the Khwarazmians) had settled.[30] The Greek and Roman writers in the times of the Achaemenians, the first Zoroastrian converts to Christianity and Islam, the Armenian writers in Sasanian times and the Muslim Arab and Perso-Arabic writers give valuable information on Zoroastrianism. Procopius's *Persian Wars* and Agathias's *Histories* are also valuable sources of information. Alongside the *Avesta* and the Pahlavi woks the singularly most important work is the *Sháhnáma* ("The Book of the Kings"), written by Firdausi in the early eleventh century C.E. in the court of Mahmud of Ghazni. On the arrival of the Zoroastrians in India a work was composed in Sanskrit in *shloka* style explaining the religion of the Iranians to the Indians. In the late sixteenth century C.E., Bahman Kaikobad composed a brief 'history' of the Parsis—the *Kisseh-e-Sanjan* or *Qesse-ye-Sanjan* ("The Story of Sanjan") which mentions the invasions of Iran by Alexander and later the Arabs and recalls the 'glorious' days of the Zoroastrians in Iran. The Jewish *Torah* mentions the Persians as the saviours of the Jews where special status is given to Cyrus. Cyrus the Zoroastrian, is also Cyrus the Messiah of the Jews besides being the King of Iran and the Universal World Empire. Herodotus's *Histories* and *The Persian Wars* and Xenophane's *Cyropaedia* are also valuable sources of information, while the Christian Gospels mention how the Magis followed the star—(literally implying followed Zarathushtra): "We have seen his star in the east" and "we have come to worship him"[31], i.e. worship the New Messiah: Jesus. In this Gnostic-subaltern and multicultural reading of Zoroastrianism one locates two intertwined legends—the Zoroastrian belief of the voyage of the soul after death and the Christian legend of Jesus's resurrection. It has been recently mentioned that the Christian legend of Jesus being resurrected on the third day is an inherent part of Zoroastrian eschatology.[32] Modern Zoroastrians believe that they are heirs to this form of multiculturalism where Zoroastrianism, Judaism, Hinduism, Buddhism, Christianity and Islam are involved in a civilizational dialogue. If this form of civilizational dialogue in the ancient world remains largely buried and forgotten, then it is also remembered by the popular masses—even if it is in kitsch form. A sect within the modern Zoroastrians—the *Ilm-e-Khshnoom*—believes that the Hindu "OM" is actually "AUM" or Ahura Mạzda. This same Zoroastrian sect holds Moses, the Buddha, Jesus, Krishna and Muhammad as being parts of the cycle of world prophets whose comings were prophesied by Zarathushtra. The spontaneous secularism of the Parsis, which led them to form the vanguard of the anti-colonial movement in the fight against British rule in India, is located in the multiculturalism in the ancient world. In fact, it is this form of multiculturalism and spontaneous secularism which forms the leitmotiv of modern India's idea of secularism.

With this brief multicivilizational history we turn to Zarathushtra's philosophy of cosmic history and human emancipation. According to Zoroastrianism there is one God—Ahura Mazda who is the unifying force of the universe. This forms the essence of his theory of the harmony of the spheres. Yet what differentiates Zarathushtra from all other teachers of monotheism is that he recognizes that the warring forces in nature have disturbed this Grand Harmony. Zoroastrianism is thus a monotheism that is dialectical. Zarathushtra calls these warring forces—the active and the reactive forces—"twin spirits" (*tā Mainyū*).[33] These primeval principles are the foundations of all reality—Nature, human society and thought. The twin spirits have existed right at the time of creation.[34] In the Zoroastrian idea of cosmic history there is a definite beginning (*pouruyē*)[35], some sort of a cosmic Big Bang that creates the entire cosmos with the conflicting forces at its centre stage. Zarathushtra gives these conflicting forces ethical connotations. One is good (*Vahyō*), while the other is bad (*Akēm*)[36], and when these two forces first met they created Life (*Gaēm*) and Not-Life (*Aijyātīm*).[37]

Not-Life is a sort of a Hegelian *Unwesen* or "non-being", what Martin Haug had called a non-reality[38]. This is the essential part of the objective logic of Zarathushtra's idea of cosmic history. If there is reality in the form of Life (one recalls Jacques Lacan's "the *Real*") on one side, there is also non-reality in the form of non-Life on the other side. In relation to this objective logic is the subjective phenomenology of Zoroastrianism. In this subjective phenomenology stands humanity that is essentially free with the eternal faculty of free choice.[39] What Zarathushtra calls the *urvan*—derived from the word "*Uru*" meaning "wide" and "*An*" implying "to breathe" and also "to exist", thus *urvan* signifying *the expansion of existence* (sometimes echoing the Indian idea of deep breathing and *the expansion of consciousness*)—is what in the language of modernity one calls: the faculty of the human mind to exercise choice. And for Zarathushtra, the *urvan* is both free as well as standing on the twin pathways. The Zoroastrian idea of freedom is sutured with this idea of the double pathways.

For Zarathushtra humanity is born free and almost (to borrow an existentialist phrase) *condemned to be free*. We say: "almost condemned" and not condemned, for in Zoroastrianism, there is no condemnation. If one could transplant Martin Heidegger's "throwness into Being" into the phrase: *throwness into freedom*, then it might not be a philosophical error. Yet this phrase has to be used with reservation. For in Zoroastrianism, unlike Heidegger's "Being" (*Sein*) and the Jewish Yahweh, there is no *Sein* from the outside who is dictating humanity. Zarathushtra thus recognizes that humanity is free, but a freedom that is grounded in an objective logic of the conflicting forces. Human freedom is thus rooted in the objective logic of history and nature. *Urvan* (the soul, or the faculty of free choice) is dialectically related to *Zurvan* (literally "Time", realized as the objective laws of nature and human history).

Since Zoroastrianism combines both the monotheistic theme of one good and just God, as well as the theme of the conflicting forces—thus the conflict of good and evil—as its central philosophical repertoire, it also raises the problem of the origins of evil. In the *Avesta*, the *Gathas* first mentions these conflicting forces in nature. While the later *Avesta* takes this theme as its constituent element—the *Vendidâd* locates its entire theme on the dual forces—it is the *Bundahišn* which looks into the question of the origins of evil. Since the theme in the *Bundahišn* (the conflict is now between *Ohrmuzd* and *Ahriman*) is found as a logical continuity of the themes in the *Avesta*, and also it is echoed in non-Iranian records of the Persians, as in Plutarch, it is safe to say that not only the war between good and evil, but also posing the question of the origins of evil becomes a central question in Zoroastrianism.

The leitmotiv in the Zoroastrian books is that the material world is good and just, but the attack of the evil one (*Angra Mainyu* later to become *Ahriman*: the Iranian devil) has defiled and corrupted the earth. But this corruption is only partial. The material world remains just and good. To protect and preserve this material world is an ethical imperative. Nature in general is celebrated in Zoroastrianism. Neither is the material world to be negated, nor is the human body to be abused. Celibacy and fasting are thus totally foreign to Zoroastrianism. In dealing with the problem of evil, one has to directly confront it. One cannot be a monk and turn one's back to the world.

Ever since the origins of evil and Ahriman's first attack on earth the Zoroastrian books claim that the conflict between good and evil is carried out—a conflict that will end *inevitably* in the total annihilation of evil. The end of evil is predetermined. It simply cannot be avoided. Zoroastrian cosmic history has three basic stages—(1) the time of creation where there is unqualified goodness, (2) the attack of *Ahriman* which brings in the stage of mixture (*Gumēzishn*), which is the conflict between good and evil, and (3) the stage of separation (*Wizārishn*) with the death of *Ahriman*. The last stage is the stage wherein dwells unqualified goodness and bliss, what is known in Zoroastrianism as *Frašō-kereti* ("restoration", "renovation" or simply "making wonderful"). Since Paradise stands at the end of history, Zoroastrianism has always been an optimistic religion.

Yet fate and history have also been cruel to them. Not only were they compelled to leave their homeland—remember that Zoroastrianism like Judaism and Hinduism and unlike Buddhism, Christianity and Islam remains rooted to one nation: in this case Iran—but also their religion, cultural history and prophet have been displaced from the memory and hearts of their fellow Iranians. A ninth century apocalyptic text views the state of affairs where not only the masses but also members of the ruling elite are depicted as changing sides and "have joined the faith and path of those heretics….."[40] Heretics (according to this text) are those that have gone onto the side of the occupying Arab forces.[41] In this ninth century apocalyptic rendering the figure of the Zoroastrian Messiah (*Saoshyant*) emerges who would fight the occupation and the colonization of Iran by the Arabs, just as the kings from ancient times fought the external enemies of Iran. Along with the Arabic-heretics are mentioned the communist Mazdakites, who "enjoined *that men* ought to have wife, children and wealth in common and in co-partnership and to relinquish from *the* use the Revelation of Mazda worship…."[42] Besides the Mazdakites and the Arabs, the Turks and the Romans are mentioned as the mortal enemies of Iran. It is in this space that the advent of the Zoroastrian saviour gained momentum.

But the figure of the coming messiah seems to be the central theme that occurs not only in Zoroastrian works. It is a theme that binds the history of Iran from the times of Zoroastrianism to Islam. So strong is the messianic theme in Iran that Richard Frye had recently mentioned that: "Someone should write a detailed study of the 'messiah in Persian history'."[43] Yet behind the narrative of the coming messiah is the tragedy of Iran in particular and Zoroastrianism in general.

Despite the triumphs, the glories, the tragedies and the messiahs, the real history of Iran from around the late fifth century C.E. to 651 C.E. was in actuality witness to an accumulation of contradictions where the Sasanian state was disintegrating with the onset of feudalism in Iran which led to the break up of the balance of forces and the class alliances in Iran. Since Zoroastrianism moves from the position of religion-in-dominance to religion-in-exile starting in 651 C.E., a brief outline of this process is necessary. While idealist theories of history point the finger of accusation to Islam (a voice that is echoed in the secular masses in Iran today who in their critique of political Islam attempt to recreate an ideology of pre-Islamic Iran), materialist historiography gives different results.[44]

The roots of the decline of Zoroastrianism lie in the political economy of the closing years of the ancient world. Pre-Islamic Iran was (and is still probably) a combination of conservative and highly innovative values,[45] a fundamental factor that made them accept Islam. It was Herodotus who had said that "no nation which so readily adopts foreign customs as the Persians."[46] That the Persians could borrow from neighbouring civilizations and adopt them for their own purposes is an important characteristic for not only understanding Iran, but also Zoroastrianism and Shiite Islam. Despite all the borrowings that the Iranians did for over four thousand years they retained the values of what they thought was Iranian. With the advent of Islam the same dialectic occurred. Islam was absorbed but the Old Iranian culture was not abandoned. A subaltern reading of Iran notes that the decline of Zoroastrianism is embedded in the class wars from the fifth century C.E. and the fight for the possession of the trade routes from Europe to Asia. Since the political economy of these histories is spoken less and the narratives of the messiahs are spoken more than necessary, Orientalism enters to fill in the missing spaces. Iran has till date been unfortunate not to have a secular revolution. Thus the binary points of view emerge: that of the Orientalists—that Islam is inherently violent—and that of messianic Islam which seems to create a salvation history emerging from its own cranium: starting with Muhammad and Ali (cousin, son-in-law of Muhammad and the first righteous Shiite imam) and culminating in the present Islamic Republic of Iran.

Iran, undoubtedly, has been defined by a tormented, almost schizophrenic cultural identity: pre-Islamic, Persian-Zoroastrian elements battling with forces and values of an Arab Islamic culture. It has been said that Persian iconographic tradition, captures this tormented, schizoid division. Like Zarathushtra's war of the conflicting twins, Iran even today represents this conflict. Yet Iran is almost compelled to adapt even conflicting cultures in order to survive. Both traditional values as well as rebellious values seem to exist comfortably in the cranium of Iran.

While historians have discussed the continuity of the Zoroastrian tradition from Zarathushtra to present times,[47] then what seems to be missing is the continuity of Iranian culture for the past four millennia.[48] The messiah is the binding link in both these continuities. While Zarathushtra and Muhammad become the messiahs par excellence for Iran, starting their own type of salvation history based on the philosophy of *messianic historicism*, yet the coming messiah (in both Zoroastrianism and Shiite Islam) seems less like Zarathushtra and Muhammad and more like a hybrid between the themes of estranged-heroism in Shakespeare's *Hamlet* and Goethe's *Faust*. It is the Shiites who recognized this almost lost heroism of the Iranian messiah. If in Shiite mythology, the messiah is the missing imam, in Zoroastrianism he comes only in the almost unrecognizable future. In the latter tradition his coming will be paralleled with the stopping of the sun for thirty days and nights.[49] At least since the ninth century, it is the messiah who will be waging war against the heretics. Political Islam picks up this theme of the war against the heretics from Sasanian Zoroastrianism.

That this theme of the fear of the infidels has moved from Sasanian and post-Sasanian Zoroastrianism to Islam has almost gone unrecognized. That Shahristani and Al-Baghdadi, both Muslim heresiographers, had picked up this theme of anti-heresy from the Sasanians has again gone unrecognized. Much has been debated on Sasanian Iran, with diametrical opposite views—one claiming that the original message of Zarathushtra was only a distant memory and the Sasanians were more involved in their own pleasure hunting while the priesthood was instrumental in building a hierarchical society (a view supported by recalling *The Letter of Tansar*); the other view is of the heroic legacy of Iran being continued by the Sasanians which ended only due to tragedy (a view not only which the Zoroastrians hold today along with the secular masses of Iran, but also which Firdausi held in his *Shâhanâma*). Even today the dominant position in Zoroastrian studies is caught between these extreme positions.

Yet one also has a contrast text to this "heretical" reading of history from "the above". In this counter-narrative it is not the politics of religion taking place, and thus not Islam and Zoroastrianism battling it out. Instead, the fundamental conflict was between the peasants and the Sasanian state. The subaltern tradition of Iran is found in this reading of class struggles in late antiquity. In this narrative of class struggles one sees the legendary left-wing Abbasid general, Abu Muslim, fighting the Umayyad Caliphate. It must be noted that Abu Muslim was regarded as both a direct descendant of Zarathushtra as well as a righteous Muslim imam, as also was his close friend and ally Ishaq "the Turk" who was considered a prophet sent by Zarathushtra. The least recorded part of Iranian history is these dual identities: Zoroastrian and Muslim best found in the second part of the communist Mazdakite movement. Likewise, Shihab al-Din Suhrawadi (1153-1234 C.E.), the neo-Platonic founder of the *Ishraqi* or the *Illuminationists*, who despite being a Muslim traced his philosophy to Zarathushtra, was also a part of this syncretic tradition, as also was Azar Kaivan, a Persian mystic (allegedly of the Sipasian sect according to the *Dasatir* a Persian work of confused origins) with distinct Zoroastrian, Hindu and Muslim ideas who came from Iran and resided in North India (Patna) in the times of Akbar the Great. The Ishraqi philosophers from Shiraz and Isfahan in Iran who combined

Zoroastrianism and Platonism with Aristotle and Islam were the living link between Iran and India, especially after they migrated to Gujarat in the early sixteenth century. Mir Siyyid Rafi'u'din Safavi (the spiritual guide to the Lodi, Mughal and the Sur dynasties), Khatib Abu'l Fazl Kazaruni and Sheikh Mubarak, the father of Abu'l-Fazl (the court philosopher of Akbar the Great) were some of the Ishraqi philosophers in India.

That the underground stream connecting not only Zoroastrian Iran with Islamic Iran, but also Iran over the centuries with India remains a strong motif binding subaltern cultures from Iran to India, as well as being the least known, is an irony. For instance, Akbar's idea of *Dîn* as the Sufi practice of *Suhl-i-Kuhl* or Universal Peace that abolished the legal difference between the Muslim and non-Muslim, which bound the entire court to the emperor, as well as enabled an egalitarian spirit in the masses, had distinct Zoroastrian echoes. The Mughal emperor who took on the role of the spiritual guide like the ancient Iranian "king of the kings" (*Shāhān Shāh*) was said to stand above all distinctions. The Mughal theory of the royal court was a replica of the Sasanian court—Akbar becomes a righteous king like Khausrau I (531-579 C.E.), and was thus, both a righteous king, as well as world philosopher and collector of world knowledge. This king-regent relation in Mughal India was not only the revival of the Sasanian policy, but the ancient Iranian system itself, since at least Jamshid (or Yima, the Indian Yama), the legendary king-prophet, who ironically hastened not only the fall from grace of not only himself and Iran, but the entire world for refusing to play the role of prophet conferred on him by Ahura Mazda. If the theme of king as regent connected Iran with Mughal India, then the theme of the fallen hero formed the crux of Iranian civilization connecting Zoroastrian Iran with Islamic Iran.[50]

There is a fourth civilizational link relating Zoroastrianism with Islam in the role of the prophet, and that is the democratic role of the messiah in Zoroastrianism which later Islam emulates. Zarathushtra is not the king. The king is Vistaspa. And in Islam the king can only be Allah. But if Sunni Islam stops with Muhammad (the last of the prophets, the cycle that was started with Adam, the first man: Adam one must stress means "humanity" in Hebrew), in Shiite Islam, God has to have a regent on earth—the imam. Ali in Shiite theology becomes not only the first righteousness imam, but also takes on the ancient Iranian role of king-prophet.[51] This is the fifth link connecting civilizations—between Zoroastrian Iran and Shiite Iran.

There are thus five links connecting the civilizations of Iran with India and Zoroastrianism with Islam:

(1) The Iranian Ishraqis with Mughal India: thus connecting Zoroastrian, Platonic and Islamic ideas with India,
(2) The Sasanian state policy of king-regent with the Mughal idea of kingship,
(3) The theme of the fallen hero—Jamshid in Zoroastrian Iran and Ali in Shiite tradition,
(4) The theme of Zarathushtra and Muhammad who are both prophets, but not kings, and
(5) Imam Ali appearing as God's regent on earth that recalls the ancient Iranian heroes.

Besides these themes that link Iran with India and Zoroastrianism with Islam, there are also two parallel paths in the continuity of Iranian culture and politics from Zoroastrian times to Islam: (1) that of the Royal Sasanian state and (2) its direct anti-thesis: the communist Mazdakite movement that erupted in Iran during the rule of monarch Kobad (487-531 C.E.) almost converting Kobad to communism and transforming the Sasanian into a socialist state. For the Mazdakites it was class justice that remained central to their political philosophy, though one must stress that the Pahlavi Books also recalled the idea of distributive justice as central to not only Sasanian Zoroastrianism, but Zoroastrianism per se[52]. Since it is not only the five points mentioned in the previous paragraph linking Zoroastrian Iran to Islamic Iran, but also the Mazdakite movement, it is necessary to briefly go into it. Unfortunately not much literature exists regarding the Mazdakites. The information that we get is from their adversaries: mainly the Perso-Arabic writers who were basically against this movement. It is only Firdausi who was somewhat sympathetic to them.

Connecting Zoroastrian Iran to Muslim Iran through the politics of the communist Mazdakites is important. O.G. von Wesendonk in 1919 in his *Die Mazdakiten* and *Die Religion der Druzen* drew parallels between the Isma'īlī sects (that emerged after the assassination of Abu Muslim) and the Mazdakite doctrines, as also between the Druzes of Lebanon and the Mazdakites.[53] Whether the Mazdakites have to be considered explicitly as Zoroastrians is again debatable. Mazdak himself appears to identify himself with "the good religion"[54]—a phrase depicting the Zoroastrian faith. Tabari also called Mazdak, "the interpreter (*al-mata'awwil*) of the Book of Zoroaster, the *Avesta*."[55] But then it is not only Mazdak the communist who is seen as the practitioner and interpreter of Zoroastrianism, but the *Avesta* is also viewed as holding communist theories:

> If fellow-believers (*hāmō daēna*), brother or friend, come to ask for money, wife or wisdom (*xratu*), he who asks for money should be given money; he who asks for wife should be given wife to marry; he who asks for wisdom should be taught the holy word.[56]

That Mazdakism was a "reformed Zoroastrianism,"[57] if not revolutionary Zoroastrianism, is more likely than it being a heresy in the form of Manicheism or some sort of non-Zoroastrian sect. Heresy was from the class point of view. According to the ideologists of Khausrau I who seized the throne from his father Kobad, Mazdakite creates blasphemy by constructing a "new religion in the world", the religion of the "community of women and of goods" where "every man is equal in the world" and where the communist Mazdakites dared to preach that the "toiling slave and Shah are equal."[58] Since the Mazdakites had gained sufficient power to abolish not only the property of the nobles, but also abolish the family system itself, there was turmoil for the Iranian ruling classes. Khausrau called on his court philosophers to counter this peasant uprising. Here, according to the ideologists of Khausrau who were mobilized to counter communism: Hormuzd of Khurra-I-Ardshír and Mihr-Ázar of Pars: Mazdak was indeed mad and "all mankind is led to Hell" by him.[59] The Mazdakites had to be destroyed by the monarchy and the clergy. They were destroyed. But the stamp of these communists could not be so easily wiped out. They went underground after Mazdak was killed.

Despite being couched in religious language, Mazdakism, was more a primitive critique of political economy, than theology. According to Firdausi, for Mazdak, philosophy had to be simple. All crimes (even sins), not to forget poverty and wars could be eliminated if a very simple solution was put into practice: *abolish private property*. This is how Firdausi represents Mazdak at the courts of Kobad converting the monarch to communism:

> Bread is the antidote for hungry men—
> An antidote not wanted by the full.....
> Should not the corn in store be put to use?
> To hunger have a million succumbed,
> Whose deaths are due to idle granaries...
> The man of empty hand
> Is equal to the man possessed of wealth...
> To right the world all men must have sufficient;
> The rich man's plenty is abominable;
> The women, goods and houses are for all....[60]

The recounting of this very important movement by Muslim writers well after it was crushed, as also well after the Sasanian state fell to the Muslim armies, means that they did definitely exist well after the execution of their legendary leader. According to Tha'ālibī it was again the politics of class that shaped the ideology of the Mazdakites. Ahura Mazda according to the Mazdakites was a communist. He created wealth for all, but human greed monopolized wealth. Private property was thus directly antithetical to the will of Ahura Mazda. Consider Tha'ālibī's account of the philosophy of the Mazdakites:

> Mazdak declared that God placed the means of subsistence (*arzaq*) on earth so that people divide them among themselves equally, in a manner that no one of them should have more than his share; but people wronged one another; the strong defeated the weak and took exclusive possession of livelihood and property. It is absolutely necessary that one take from the rich for giving to the poor, so that all become equal in wealth. Whoever possesses an excess of property, women or goods, he has more right than the other.[61]

And when the philosophy of God being a communist seized the masses, they not only demanded the public distribution of wealth, but also seized the granaries. This led to the onslaught of the state on the revolutionary peasants. Left-wing Zoroastrianism was crushed by the Sasanian state. Despite Khausrau I's driving the Mazdakites underground, they were never totally annihilated. If the Sasanian state persecuted them, then their fate under the Arabs was even worse. But their remaining in the underground and taking different religious identities remains the central part of the great motor force in the transformation from Zoroastrian Iran to Islamic Iran. The primary theological question for the Mazdakites was: *If God is just, then is he for the poor or for the rich?*

It must be noted that besides the Mazdakites and the Mazdeans or the orthodox Zoroastrians of what is called the "Zoroastrian Church"[62] founded by the first Sasanian monarch Ardashīr Papakan (226-241 C.E.), there were also other sects of Zoroastrians in Iran like the *Gayômarteans* (who believed in "the first man": *Gayômart*)[63], the *Zurvanists* (who believed that *Zurvan Akarana* or "Infinite Time" was the father of the "twins", i.e. the father of both God and the devil), the *Zurvanist materialists* (who believed in time, independent of the existence of God, as the motor force of history), [64] the *Maskhiyya* or the *Transformationists* (who believed that evil has to be transformed into goodness, and who also believed that the origins of the devil Ahriman lay in God)[65] and the subaltern Zoroastrianism of the non-Iranian lands (the *an-aryas*) most notably the Kurds. When Islam came to Iran it "smashed Zoroastrianism", as Zaehner says, "as a national power, but also destroyed it as a cultural influence..."[66] But behind this messianic *smashing* lay the crisis of the ideological power of the Zoroastrian clergy, quite often called the "Zoroastrian Church". The latter was, as Zaehner says, "found wanting."[67] Interesting Karl Marx in his *Notes on Indian History* says that, "Mohammedianism made rapid progress among the *Persians* than among the *Hindus* because there priest class was lowest and most degraded class, whereas in India it was the most powerful political agent in the Commonwealth."[68] The date however that Marx makes in these diaries is 714[69], well after the collapse of the Sasanians.

But no serious centralized resistance came from the Sasanian state itself. The authoritarian nature of the Sasanian state and the class-stratified nature of Iranian society led not only to the collapse of the agnatic Sasanian family in control of Iran, but also to the Persian Empire. Resistance to the new agnatic family in control of Iran—the Umayyad—came in multiple forms, the most prominent being the birth of Shiite Islam. One probable explanation of the lack of resistance from the Sasanian state is the role of the tragic hero in Iranian history (best exemplified in the pre-Islamic narrative of Rustum and Sohrab). For the Arabs victory had nothing to do with religion. It was purely materialistic—the rule over a more developed civilization. The gains, again, were economical. Nor was the Umayyad Caliphate interested in matters of theological concerns. But after the coming to power of the governor of Syria Mu'awiyah as the Muslim Caliph and the murder of Ali and his sons Hassan and Hussain by the Caliphate the revolutionary essence of Islam (which it may have picked up in diluted form from the Mazdakites) was severely compromised. It must be noted that the Shiites never accepted the first three of the Muslim caliphs: Abu Bakr, followed by 'Umar and 'Uthman and till the rule of the Shah of Iran, Nadir Shah (1729 C.E.), publicly abused them. That Ali gripped the imagination of Muslim Iran was derived probably from an Iranian nationalist myth that he married Sherbanu, the daughter of the last Sasanian emperor, Yazdegird III and fathered Hassan and Hussain from her, thus combining both Iranian royalty and the New Messiah.

Civilizationally two prominent incidents happen (besides the birth of a new Utopia and also the synthesis of the Persian and Arabic languages giving way to probably one of the most beautiful languages of the world: Modern Persian)—left-wing Mazdakites in the times of Zoroastrian Iran changed to Shiite Islam of the subaltern masses, and the idea of the ideal Zoroastrian state as enunciated by Ardashīr—namely the doctrine of the identity of the state and religion—was taken over as the model state by later Islamic governments.[70] This idea of the *sacrosanctity of the state*, which even today contemporary orthodox Islam believes in, is paradoxically borrowed from Sasanian Zoroastrianism. One can argue that political theology has nothing to do with the *Koran*, just as it had nothing to do earlier with the *Avesta*. Yet political theology despite the thinking of the three great messiahs, Zarathushtra, Jesus and Muhammad, did come marching in the world. Revolutions and Utopias it seems are closely bound to counterrevolutions and Distopias. This is how the classical anti-secular doctrine of the unity of religion and politics was formulated by the first Sasanian monarch Ardashīr:

> Know that kingship and religion are twin brothers, no one of which can be maintained without the other. For religion is the foundation of the state, and the state is the guardian of religion. The state cannot subsist without its foundation, and religion cannot exist without its guardian. For that which has no guardian is lost, and that which has no foundation crumbles.....Know that there can never be in one kingdom both a secret chief in religion and a manifest chief in kingship without the chief in religion snatching away that which is in the hands of the chief in kingship. For religion is the foundation and kingship is the pillar, and the possessor of the foundation has more claim to the whole building than the possessor of the pillar.[71]

It ought to be noted that it is this pre-Islamic doctrine that also served as the basis of contemporary right-wing politics in Iran. Islam owes much to Iran and the Zoroastrians. Not only is the mandatory five times prayer of the faithful in Islam, a central Zoroastrian practice, but also the ideas of the bridge of judgement (*Chinvatō Peretu* in Zoroastrianism, *Al-Sirat* in Islam), righteousness, judgement, heaven and hell, along with folk poetry and legends of pre-Islamic Iran, art and architecture, the *Waqf* Board in charge of religious property and the political economy of taxation developed by Khausrau I after the defeat of the communist Mazdakites (the *jizyah* tax system), became central parts of the political economy and culture of Islam. The Islamic exaltation to Allah (*Bismillah Ir-Rahman, Ir-Rahim,* "In the name of God, the Merciful and Compassionate") is said to be derived from the Zoroastrian phrase: "*Pad nam I Yazdan,*"[72] while the Avestan archangels: *Haurvatāt* ("Perfection") and *Ameretatāt* ("Immortality") are metamorphosizied as the Koranic *Harut* and *Marut*. Probably one of the most ignored themes in world history has been the ignorance on the part played, by not only the Persians in the development of Islam, but of Zoroastrian ideas in the formation of Islamic eschatology. The Jewish, Christian and Islamic ideas of one God, the prophet, heaven and hell, resurrection and the end of the world are all Zoroastrian ideas. The exilic Jews learnt of these ideas in Achaemenian Iran (559-330 B.C.E.) and via the Jews, the early Christians and the Zoroastrian sage: Bēhzād (soon to become Salman Farsi, or "the wise Persian", one of Prophet Muhammad's close companions), these ideas crystallized in the latest and the most dynamic of all monotheistic religions, Islam. The Perso-Greco-Arabic sciences and philosophies that developed in Islamic times, under the Caliph Haroun-al-Rashid, were built on the model of the Sasanian *Jundi-Shapur*. But like the Oedipal myth, the Zoroastrian parent fades away with the birth of this new child.

Just as in the metamorphosis of commodities, where the origin of commodity production is lost, so too in the history of West Asia, Zoroastrianism faded away. There are two interpretations of the fate of Zoroastrianism, post-651 C.E. One that a militant Islam ravages all that resisted it, this being the favourite theme of not only the Orientalists, but of modern day Islamophobes. The other theme is that a mutation took place wherein Shiite Islam, as a synthesis of Zoroastrianism and Islam, was born. Since the old idealist theories of history are usually evoked to explain the rise of Islam, and since the Mazdakite movement in particular and the historical materialist theory of class struggles do not come up in the field of scientific explanation, more often than not, the anti-Islamic school comes up in explaining the history of religions.

What happens in this idealist explanation is that the idea of the conflict between good and evil as the central part of Zoroastrianism, where the notion that evil in the form of the (hellish) devil (Ahriman) has attacked the earth, is transformed into the apocalyptic theory that evil in the form of the (Arab) devil has attacked Iran. Two images come up. The first is that of Alexander's (since then known by the Zoroastrianism as *gusastag* or the "accursed") infamous attack on Iran, and the second is that of the Arab invasion with the rise of Islam. In both cases, one sees the burning of the Persian books and the supposed destruction of "Iranian Reason." The Zoroastrian apocalypse is now born. And since these images are again being evoked, especially after the rise to power of the previous right-wing president of Iran, Mahmoud Ahmadinejad, and also since the ideology of the pan-Iran movement that is actively constructing a pre-Islamic past of an alleged "golden age"; the politics of the Persian apocalypse needs to be mentioned. Zoroastrianism is not only a religion that once existed that held sway over a large part of the world. Zoroastrianism is the religion that will again grip the imagination of Iran. The repressed, simply had to return. It was Sigmund Freud who had taught us this.

And yet the image of the devil attacking Iran is not static. The devil that is now to attack Iran is no longer the Arab neighbour. The devil comes from across the Atlantic Ocean. Alexander, now reborn as the USA, as the student of Aristotle, becomes not only the student of Western Reason, but becomes the father of Western Imperialism. This becomes the central part of the Iranian apocalypse. In this narrative, Western Reason is actually Persian Wisdom that is robbed from Iran. After all, the Middle Persian Zoroastrian books—most notable the ninth century C.E., encyclopaedic *Dînkard*, Vol. IV—claim that one copy of the *Avesta* was burnt by Alexander while the other copy was given to Aristotle. What Aristotle did to the *Avesta* is never told. But since clear Persian themes of governance emerge in Aristotle's *Politics* and since themes that Aristotle worked with emerge in the *Dînkard,* one possible interpretation is that much lies in Aristotle than his own ingenuity.[73]

But if the original text of Zoroastrianism is the *Avesta,* accompanied by the commentaries and interpretations known as the *Zand* (with the Middle Persian or Pahlavi works forming the philosophical and historical corpus of Zoroastrianism), there is also the distinct philosophical impact of Zoroastrianism on the history of world philosophy that is understated in mainstream discourses. The history of Western Philosophy since Augustine, has nothing almost to say about Zarathushtra (with the exceptions of Hegel and Nietzsche), just as Christianity (with the formation of the Pauline Church) has nothing to say about Zoroastrianism, even though the *Bible* says Cyrus the Persian was a prophet of the Jews ("Lord's anointed one") that it was the magus—the followers of Zarathushtra—who greeted the baby Jesus in Bethlehem.[74]

This fate of Zoroastrianism—from the zenith of World Empire to minority community—can be best understood in Nietzsche's rendering. According to Nietzsche's magnum opus *Also sprach Zarathustra,* Zarathushtra has gone underground.[75] He now lives, as Nietzsche claims, in the underworld (*Unterwelt*).[76] This rendering of Nietzsche is both subversive and pessimistic. It is subversive, for according to Nietzsche, Zarathushtra (remember he gets his name—"he of the Golden Light"—from the sun) rises like the sun only to set in the evening. This setting of the sun implies that he has gone into the underground in order to give light there. Thus his going to the underworld is to give light to this *Unterwelt.* Remember light is central to Zoroastrianism. Since light has gone to this underworld, or even since reason has gone in the underworld, one thus has to descend into this underworld in order to understand Zarathushtra. But the underworld, even metaphorically, is anathema to the Zoroastrians. Instead it is light which forms one of the main pillars of Zoroastrian civilization. And yet the state of going into the underground cannot entirely be a mistaken idea. For how could the Zoroastrians who not only ruled a great part of the world, and even till the fifteenth century in Iran number in millions suddenly regress into a minority community? How could Zoroastrianism after influencing the births of Judaism, Greco philosophy, Christianity and Islam suddenly disappear into the memory of forgetfulness? How does this forgetfulness of Zarathushtra operate?

If the birth and growth of Zoroastrianism has been in Iran, then the sustenance has been in India. It is clearly speculative as to what would have happened to Zoroastrianism if the Persians had not come to India. For one thing there was more than one flight from Iran—the first being the Persian nobles accompanying the then young prince Peroj (the son of the last Zoroastrian monarch Yazdegird III) to China. But they have disappeared into history, though traces of fire temples have been left behind in China. There are remains of fire temples in Kaifeng and Zhenjiang in China which existed till the thirteenth century C.E.. How Peroj's group seems to have disappeared into history is not yet known. Since Zoroastrian apocalyptic texts mention the future Zoroastrian saviour: the famed Shah Bahram Varjevand who is reputed to cross "the frontiers of Kâvulastan"[77], it is said that he would come from China in the name of A-luo-han (the Chinese name of Yazdegird III's son Wahram who was given refuge in China).[78] One possibility is that the Chouhans of North India may have something to do with this missing group of Persians. For the name "Chouhan" is composed of two Chinese names: "Chou" and "Han". That the Rajputs have less to do with the myth of the descent from the solar dynasties, and more to do with the Indo-Iranians (Scythians, Kushans and the Huns) is well known from the times of A.M.T. Jackson and D.R. Bhandarkar. But there is also one more interesting observation brought about at the beginning of the twentieth century when it was said that the great Maratha warrior king Shivaji had descended from the Sasanian king Khausrau I.[79] Though the present Zoroastrians in India trace their genealogy from the flight from Iran to Gujarat, there have also been observations of Zoroastrians in Tughliqpur in North India in the late fourteenth century indicating that either there was migration from Gujarat to North India, or a different group of Zoroastrians came from Iran and landed in North India. Timur in 1398 had observed what he called a "perverse creed" of fire-worshippers who believed in two gods, one called Yazdan (the good god) and the other Ahriman (the bad god).[80] But besides these rather vacuous spaces there is a more definite history noted—the flight of the Zoroastrians from Iran to Gujarat.

It is this flight of the Zoroastrians to India that opens a new chapter in the history of Zoroastrianism. This voyage to India is the next part in the history of Zoroastrianism. Whether Zoroastrianism would be alive today if not for this group of fleeing Persians cannot be safely ascertained. For parallel to their voyage, there was fierce resistance from their Iranian brethren in Iran. The most heroic of the resistances was one of the *Khurramiyaya* (the followers of Babak al-Khurramī's "the religion of pleasure" in the ninth century C.E.) a distinct left-wing group (an offshoot of the communist Mazdakites) who had launched fierce resistance to the Arab rulers.[81] What one gets is at least two distinct histories—one the flight to India the other the birth of Shiite religion—a marriage between Gnostic Zoroastrianism and the followers of Ali—a religion, as we mentioned, which also probably adopted, at least partially, a part of the ideology of left-wing Zoroastrianism of the revolutionary Mazdakites. The *Kizilbash* ("Red Heads") who were instrumental in the foundation of the Safavid dynasty of Iran, and followers of their Sufi Grandmaster Haydar head of the *Safawiyya Sufi Order* were the spiritual and political heirs of the Mazdakites and the *Khurramiyaya*. It is thus no surprise that the modern Shiites of Iran even today place the communist motif of class conflict [in the Shiites the principal conflict is between the *Mostazafin* (the oppressed) and the *Mostakberin* (the oppressors)] as the leitmotiv of their religious ideology.

After the assassination of the last Sasanian emperor Yazdegird III in 651 C.E., on orders of the governor of Marv, Mahu-i-Suri, political power passed on to a new political centre—the newly Islamized Arabs who under Islam move from the position of economic and political periphery to the centre of history itself. In Iran the impact of the new religious ideology was itself complex. According to Mary Boyce this was the beginning of the "dark centuries" for Zoroastrianism.[82] Yet how conversions operate in the matrix of ideologies-in-dominance has yet to be written. That religion is not merely an article of faith, but also a matter of ideology is not yet clarified in Iranian studies, especially in the transformation of Zoroastrianism into Islam. "Conversions" in Iran operated in the matrix of the changing ruling classes and the ruling ideologies of these new classes. The question of forced conversions after the defeat of the Sasanians and after the advent of Muslim rule is a hard fact which theological states have enforced on the masses. Yet force is always mixed with consent, the Ideological State Apparatus almost inevitably takes over from the Repressive State Apparatus. But, most of all, fact has always been mixed with romantic fiction. Instead it was the change in the balance of forces at the time of Khausrau I (and well before the advent of Islam) with the birth of a rational bureaucracy and a rational tax system that gave rise to the new bureaucracy that did not need any religious allegiances to sustain its economic and political power. The first to change their religious alliances were members of the bureaucracy and ruling elites, in contrast to the middle landed gentry (*dihqāns*) or minor aristocrats like Firdausi who fiercely kept the faith of Zarathushtra alive, and even after 'converting' did not lose their Persian faith. The Arabs after their swift victories over the Sasanian forces kept the same bureaucracy to rule Iran. Richard Frye states that the collapse of the Sasanians was due to the excessive wars that they had mainly with the Byzantines which exhausted both the economy of Iran as well as its armed forces.[83] That the destiny of Zoroastrianism was so closely woven with botched up military campaigns of the Sasanians and the excessive taxation imposed on the peasants and the merchants has been noted.[84] At least till the first decade of the seventh century C.E. (when Zoroastrian power was at its peak) the military campaigns seemed to be going successfully for the Persian forces. Heraclius seized power from Maurice the Byzantine monarch and father-in-law of Khausrau II which gave an excuse for the latter to resume conflict with the Byzantines. Antioch, Jerusalem and Alexandria were taken back into the Persian Empire. The Persians were then knocking at the doors of Constantinople. But swiftly the fortunes of the Persian forces changed for the worse. In 628 C.E. Heraclius defeated the Sasanian forces and captured the royal palace but Khausrau II refused to make peace which forced his generals to overthrow and then kill him.[85] On hindsight it could be said that it was better that the Sasanian state policy would have been the policy of the kinship of the generals and the throne, than between religion and the king.

The transformation of Zoroastrian Iran into Muslim Iran takes a long time with clear Zoroastrian themes being imbibed into Islam. The messiah is the theme that binds the discontinuous worlds of Zoroastrianism and Islam. Zarathushtra became Moses and Abraham, Jamshid became Solomon and Noah, the coming saviour in Zoroastrianism became the missing imam, and the Book: the *Avesta* became the *Koran*. One of the dominant features is that *Persianized Islam*—or "the Persian conquest of Islam"[86] was born with the meeting of these two prophetic religions. The deepest transformation was in the economic mode of production where Iran of the ancient world and the empire was being transformed into feudalism. But if the deepest transformation was from the ancient world into feudalism (which already began probably in Parthian times, though one must keep the idea of the Asiatic mode of production and a highly centralized state in mind), there was also the transformation in the ruling elite family of Iran from the Sasanians who ruled from 226 to 651 C.E. to the Umayyad dynasty (651-750 C.E.). But more than these above noted transformations the most ignored and important transformation was in the subaltern masses—the transformation from materialism, atheism, scepticism, heresy and infidelity to materialism, atheism, scepticism, heresy and infidelity. This part of Iran's history has probably not yet been written. But if in Iran a complex matrix was being created—the best phrase could be the *Zoroastrianization of Islam*—in India the newly arrived Persians would want to keep the memory of the *Avesta* alive. But here the irony and unintended consequences of history operates. For the Zoroastrians who had parted ways with the early Hindus in probably the Second Wave of the Indo-Iranian Migrations—the clearest stamp of the parting of the ways of these two Indo-Iranian people is stated in the mythical conflict between the *asuras* and the *devas*—now returned to the company of the *deva* (devil) worshipping Hindus. If Darius's inscriptions mention the stamping of *deva* worship from Iran (the *Vendidâd* mentions how to drive away the evil demons headed by the much hated *Indra*: the demon of war and destruction),[87] a theme repeated in Sasanian Iran despite both Achaemenian and Sasanian Iran's close proximity to the Indians, then the descendants of Darius and the people of the book: the *Vendidâd*, had to come to the same *deva* worshipping land. And it is in India—the land that the *Avesta* says wherein dwell not only demons but which was also created by Ahura Mazda[88]—that they make their new home. And it is this new home that the memory of their religion is kept alive. *Indra*, it seems, would protect the Zoroastrians.

India, undoubtedly, became the home where the flame of the religion is kept alive. But more than the alleged self-proclaimed inherent secular nature of India and Hinduism, it is the absence of messianic theology in India combined with what Karl Marx once called "idyllic village communities,"[89] that left the space for autonomy for the Persians to survive in India without any fear of state-sponsored persecution. The history of the Zoroastrians from the time of the arrival to the time of the British has yet to be written in detail. It is from around the fifteenth century onwards with the development of mercantile capital in Gujarat that the voices of the Parsis begin to be heard. The names of Maneck Changa at the court of Humayun and then the legendary high priest Dastur Meherji Rana (who allegedly 'converted' Akbar the Great to Zoroastrianism) stand out with the flowering of Mughal rule in India. Meherji Rana became one of the court philosophers at Fatepur Sikri, soon to be followed by his son Kaikobad Mahyar who served the emperor Jehangir. Whether Rana gave an Ishraqi account of Zoroastrianism to Akbar is not clear. Bada'uni, a Muslim scholar not known for his liberal views, mentions in the *Muntakhab-al-Tawarikh* how Akbar, "openly worshipped the sun and the fire by prostrations, and (how) the courtiers were ordered to rise when the candles and lamps were lit."[90] Akbar then had a fire temple constructed and gave his favourite courtier the Ishraqi philosopher Abu'l Fazl orders to tend to it. That the voices—both the secular voices in the field of trade and commerce and the philosophical—are heard since the times of the Mughals testifies to the fact that the Zoroastrians were always comfortable with societies based on developed forces of production.

After the Mughals, it was when they came into contact with the Europeans in the early years of the British rule in India that the next chapter opened for the Parsis. If the first chapter of the contact with capitalist Europe was trade, the next one was ideology. This chapter of the contact with capitalist Europe includes the discovery of the science of historical linguistics in Europe, the ideological attack by John Wilson on the Zoroastrian faith and the rethinking of the Parsi faith in the era of colonialism. With the help of the newly acquired disciplines of philology and historical linguistics the Zoroastrians were able to rethink the *Avesta*, a rethinking that transformed the ritualistic interpretation to a secular rendering, a secularization that would propel them as the pioneers of the spirit of modernity in Western India. The second important part of the encounter of the Parsis with the Europeans is the absorption of European modernity. It is here that the two cultures of the Persians and the Europeans met. Two prominent effects would be seen: the development of a middle class and the formation of a new industrial national bourgeoisie.

But there would also be a scholastic impact of the meeting of the Zoroastrians with the Europeans—the discovery of what Zarathushtra 'really' meant, independent of Zoroastrian liturgy. Though Zoroastrianism caught the imagination of the European scholars since Anqutil du Perron's (1731-1805) 'discovery' of the *Avesta* in Surat in Gujarat in 1759, it was with the development of the sciences of philology and historical linguistics that the content of the *Avesta* was 'known' to the Europeans. What they found was (to their great dismay) a civilization far predating both the Greeks and Christianity. William Jones's famous lecture at the formation of the Asiatic Society in Bengal in the late eighteenth century where he proclaimed that a new world of Sanskrit and Persian joined in the cultural map of Latin and Greek in the great civilizations of antiquity was almost a kind of a cultural revolution that would soon brew in the study of the Eastern nations.

This sighting of an almost hidden continent would soon challenge the hegemony of feudal and capitalist Europe. After all: What does one do with civilizations far predating the Judeo-Greco civilization? It is a question that has repeatedly emerged, one of the most important voices being that of Nietzsche soon to be followed by Max Horkheimer and Theodor Adorno's *Dialectic of Enlightenment*. The hegemony of Europe and Western Reason which was challenged from Europe at least since Voltaire would find newer voices.

Meanwhile in India the impact of English education in India was being felt by the middle of the nineteenth century. Dadabhai Naoroji was the pioneer of the social reform movement followed by K. R. Cama and Behram Malabari. It is this moment that gave rise to the class of organic intellectuals, emancipated from ritualistic Zoroastrianism that gave an impetus to the processes of modernization in India. What happened was a radical interpretation of the categories of the Parsi faith. Spenta Mainyu, the Zoroastrian progressive force, which was usually interpreted as the "Holy Spirit", was re-transcribed as the force of progression, and in the era of early industrial capitalism became the political economy of producing wealth. It literally became surplus value.

While a group calling itself "The Young Bombay" developed in Bombay where issues like widow remarriage among Hindus, education against superstition, etc., were raised, a corresponding ideological need to be aware of the basics of Zoroastrianism was felt by the Parsis as it was under constant attack by the English missionaries. The interaction with the educated English elites and the attacks on the Parsis by the Christian missionaries impelled the Parsis to rethink their faith in the light of modern European studies. It is at this time that affirmative action amongst the Parsis came into being with reference to the understanding of Zoroastrianism. While two of Wilson's Parsi students converted to Christianity there was a storm raised amongst the Parsis including a bribe allegedly offered by Sir Jamshedji Jeejeebhoy to the new converts to Christianity, as also an open threat of revolt by the Parsis against the British government. At the same time a Parsi journal the *Rahunuma-e-Zartoshi* (1842) came into being followed by the school for Zoroastrian studies (actually a seminary for Zoroastrian priests) the *Mulla Feroze Madrassa* (1854) where the German philologist Martin Haug teaching then at Poona (now Pune) was asked to be its director in 1861. Then capital flowed in for the scientific study of Zoroastrianism and along it was born both orthodox and liberal newspapers and associations: *Rahe Rast* ("The True Way"), *Suryadaya* ("Sunrise"), both orthodox newspapers, along with the orthodox reform association, *Rahe Rastnumae Zarathustrian Sabha* and the liberal paper *Rast Goftar*. With them came the great Parsi scholars: K.R. Cama, Peshotan Sanjana, Kavasji Kanga, Jivanji Mody, G.K. Nariman, S.K. Hodiwalla and M.N. Dhalla. It was on this site of contradictions, that if not, modern Zoroastrian scholarship, at least modern Zoroastrian ideology emerged.

Sometime in the 1840s, Haug worked on his magnum opus which seriously began challenging the cultural hegemony of the West. According to Haug not only did the *Bible* mention the Persians (we have already mentioned this), but also the Greek philosophers actually borrowed from the Zoroastrians. The most famous (rather infamous borrowing) is Plato's notion of the "Idea", which (according to Haug) was nothing but a transplantation of the Zoroastrian *Fravashi* ("the Transcendental Essence") into Greek thought. What is inferred is that philosophical thought (not merely Greek idealism or Plato's metaphysics), but *philosophy as philosophy* was born in Iran and then taken over by the Greeks. After Haug it was

Richard Reitzenstein who continued this reversal of Western hegemony claiming for a Persian origin of world civilization. After all, why did the Greeks themselves mention Zarathushtra (Theopompous's *On Miraculous Things*, Hermippus's *On the Magis*, Plato in the *Alcibiades* and Aristotle in the now lost *Peri Philosophia*) from whom many Greek thinkers—Pythagoras noted to be one famous 'student' of Zarathushtra—learnt their first lessons in philosophy? And if Plato's "Idea", the central part of not only Greek metaphysics, but also Western civilization from mathematics to theology and politics, was an Iranian borrowing; then is not also Plato's celebrated philosopher-king none but Cyrus the Great?

Maybe this idea that Iran stood at the sole centre of philosophical wisdom—an idea that derives from Eisler's *Weltenmatel und Himmelszelt* (1910)—is more than exaggerated, probably the invention of Romantic Iranianism. The truth is that there was a melting pot where Egyptian, Babylonian, Iranian, Indian and Greek thoughts met where at least the "Idea" (as being a central part of mathematics, theology and politics) was created. But what the discovery of Zarathushtra did in Europe was to borrow Duchesne-Guillemin's phrase: "emancipate(d) modern man from Christianity."[91] It taught Europe that well before Christianity taught the first lessons of primal sin and enforced the psychology and politics of guilt on the whole world, Iran was well steeped in the lessons of truth speaking, laughing and shooting well with arrows. Christian Europe's fable that life began with the Biblical prophets would be a myth that was now bursting at its seams.

Since the Greeks (as also the Romans) did mention Zarathushtra almost in terms of a parent figure in philosophical reasoning (despite the view that the non-Greco, non-Roman world was said to be comprised of barbarians—the dominant ideology not only of Herodotus but also Aristotle in his *Politics*) the understanding of the philosophical exchange of ideas between Iran and Greece becomes necessary. It has now been documented that both the ideas of Zarathushtra as well as his direct mentioning appears from Anaximander and Heraclitus to Plato and Aristotle. This historical voice of Zarathushtra emerging in Greek and Roman literature from Hermippus, Theopompus, Clement of Alexandria and Xanthus of Lydia, and from Plato and Aristotle to Plutarch, Diogenes Laeritus, Pliny, Aristoxenus, Eudemus and Amnianus Marcellinus; necessitates the re-reading of Zarathushtra as a world philosopher. This reading of Zarathushtra as world philosopher then is related to the central problems of world philosophy: "How is one to understand the origins of monotheism, as also the questions: *What is righteousness? What is justice? What is courage?*" Further: "Would monotheism logically give way to the Papal theology and the Dark Ages of religious persecutions or can there be a humanist reading of monotheism freed from theological hegemony? Would monotheism be more of the innermost desires and hopes of humanity than the quest for dominance? In this case would one understand humanity not so much as the Aristotelian *zoon politikon,* but as the being that desires Utopia? Or would monotheism actually be about the death of God—that Nietzsche talked of where God's brief history as outlined in the *Genesis* where God created life on the first day and on the seventh day rested never to get up ever again? Is monotheism then about the eternal rest of God?"

Cosmic History: The World As Contradictions and Paradise

The sword of Damocles always hangs over the heads of monotheism and the messianic heroes. For if God is indeed good, then from where comes evil? Is God good, but not fully potent? Or is God potent and not fully good? According to Zoroastrianism, Ahura Mazda ("the Lord of Wisdom" sometimes also transcribed as "the Wise Lord") is the One True God, filled with light, wisdom and goodness and the giver of all life. The harmony of the spheres is manifested from this life-force. Ahura Mazda is omnipotent and omniscient, but most importantly Ahura Mazda is ever good. Neither does wrath, nor destruction or death emanate from Ahura Mazda.[92] Ahura Mazda is also the first principle in Zoroastrianism. Being the sole creator, Ahura Mazda is also considered as the Highest One and the One Supreme and self-reliant Being.[93] This is the first site in the Zoroastrian idea of the creation of the universe. Now God, for the Zoroastrians, is not a purely transcendent God, estranged from creation. Instead the Zoroastrian idea of God is pantheistic, where God realizes itself in nature.

So accompanying God are the "the Bountiful Immortals" (*Amesha Spentas*) and the archangels in the form of "the Worshipful Beings" (*Yazatas*). The *Amesha Spentas* and the *Yazatas* are the manifestations of this Supreme Essence. All nature (in fact nature as Nature)—the entire cosmos—from the sun, the moon and the stars, to the earth, vegetation, humanity and animals are included in the *Amesha Spentas* and the *Yazatas*. This comprises the Harmony of the Spheres.

God is the Essence and the "the Bountiful Immortals" (*Amesha Spentas*) and "the Worshipful Beings" (*Yazatas*) are the forms of appearance of this Essence. Ahura Mazda is One and united—in fact it is the unifying principle of the entire cosmos. In contrast to this "One" are the "manifoldness" of "the Bountiful Immortals" (*Amesha Spentas*) and "the Worshipful Beings" (*Yazatas*). This form of appearance and manifestation of Ahura Mazda permeate both the material and the ideal worlds. This is how the order of the *Amesha Spentas* goes: *Vohu Manah* ("the Good Mind"), *Asha Vahista* ("the Cosmic Law of Nature"), *Khashathra Vairya* ("The Kingdom"), *Spenta Armaiti* ("Devotion"), *Haurvatāt* ("Perfection") and *Ameretatāt* ("Immortality").

The *Yazatas* comprise as if the second site of Nature: the Transcendental Essence (*Fravashi*), the endless light (*Angra Raochah*), the sky (*Asman*), atmosphere (*Vāta*), the sun (*Hvare-khshaeta*), the moon (*Māonh*), fire (*Āar*), water (*Āpān*), the shooting star (*Tishtrya*), the earth (*Zam*), the soul of the earth (*Geush Urvan*), Friendship (*Mithra*), peace and joy (Rāman), good blessing (*Ashi*), rectitude (*Arshtāt*), hearing (*Sraosha*), brightness (*Rashnu*), conscience (*Daēnā*), victory (*Verethraghna*) and the bountiful word (*Manthra Spenta*).

The basic structure of the universe is structured as stated as above. This basic structure comprises the two worlds—the material (*gaēthya*) and the spiritual (*manahya*) worlds.

The material and the spiritual worlds—the earth and the astral heavens, the body and the soul—are not fragmented, dual worlds, but concretely structured. The material and the spiritual realms are thus concretely bound together. For Zoroastrianism, the conflict in nature is not between matter and spirit, the body and the mind. Neither is the material world nor the human body evil. In fact it is the direct contrast—the material world as well as the human body is good. The entire material world—the creation from the sky and the earth to fire and water, humanity and animals—has to be venerated. Once this structure of nature is understood then its mechanism and functioning can be highlighted.

As was noted above, the conflict of opposite forces is the central part of Zoroastrian cosmic history. To borrow Nietzsche's phrase, Zarathushtra sees in this grand conflict "the actual wheel in the working of things."[94] The origins of this dual force and the cosmic wheel, which was Zarathushtra's idea of the motor force of natural history, is debated seriously since the Sasanian philosophers, followed by the Armenian and Syrian critics of Zoroastrianism, culminating in the last century by the debates of the European Iranianists. Since Zoroastrianism states that from the beginning of the universe, there are the "twin forces" (diametrically opposite to one another and always in a state of conflict), it was deduced that Zoroastrianism is a dualism. The history of dualism itself has a history starting with the Chaldean *Oracles*, then running to Parmenides in ancient Greece and then running from Christianity, Mani and the Indian *Sankhya* philosophers to Rene Descartes, Thomas Hyde (who coined the term *dualismus*), Pierre Bayle, Leibniz and Christian Wolff. If Zarathushtra's ideas are echoed in Western philosophy in this form of dualistic philosophy, then it is most certainly a mistaken way by wrongly transposing Zarathushtra's warring twins into the vocabulary of dualism. The interpretation of Zoroastrianism being a dualist philosophy begins with the first Christian criticism of Zoroastrianism from Armenia in the works of Eznik of Kolb and Elišē Vardapet and then by the Syrians Theôdor Bar Konai and Yohânnan bar Penkayê. That Eznik's work was more political and ideological than philosophical is testimony to the anti-Sasanian propaganda that the Christians were doing to undermine Iran. Likewise Shahristani made the same mistake in misrepresenting Zoroastrianism with the triumph of Islam. In contrast to the idea of reading Zarathushtra as dualism, it was Goethe who had grasped the tragic character of the dialectic in a better manner:

> Two souls, alas, are housed in my breast,
> And each will wrestle for the mastery there.[95]

We shall read this mistaken idea of dualism and claim that a Spinozist reading grants dualist ontology to Zoroastrianism, while a Hegelian reading allows other alternatives that do not enter the rubric of dualism. That Hegel comes so close to Zarathushtra's thought—in the Introduction to the *History of Philosophy* he grants Zarathushtra the place of the first dialectician in world history—as also that Frederick Engels's *Dialectics of Nature* and Lenin's *Philosophical Notebooks* echoing Zarathushtra's idea of the conflicting forces in nature, society and human thought has almost never been recognized. The slippage into dualism is thus well understood.

This is how the Spinozist rendering of the categories of Zoroastrianism goes. According to this version, Ahura Mazda or God is the *substance* and the causa sui: that which exists in itself and does not need anything for its existence. Now this substance has two *attributes*—good and evil: *Spenta Mainyu* and *Angra Mainyu,* while the *Amesha Spentas* and the *Yazatas* are the modes of this self-caused substance. Since God as substance has good and evil as its attributes, then dualism is the necessary result.[96] But this would be at variance with the Zoroastrian idea of the *total separation* of good and evil. Good and evil according to Zoroastrianism can never meet, except in states of conflict.

In contrast to the Spinozist rendering of Ahura Mazda is the Hegelian one. Here good and evil are similar to Hegel's "Being" (*Sein*) and "Non-being" (*Unwesen*), or even better *Nichts* or "nothing."[97] While goodness is solid like Being, evil is an *Unwesen* and a *Nichts,* almost an emptiness and a type of estrangement from Being. Since both *Unwesen* and *Nichts* signify a "lack"[98], *evil here is undestood as a "lack" of goodness.* Yet one must insist, in Zoroastrianism, evil has an ontological presence. Evil as *Unwesen, Nichts* and *lack* becomes some sort of dark matter and a cosmic black hole that devours the solidness of Being.

From this *Ur*-contradiction: Being and Non-being, all opposites of the universe unfold. Ahriman, the Iranian devil, becomes the nothingness and the master of estrangement. He is also the champion of the "lack" and the political economy of scarcity. In this maze of dialectical opposites (remember that the entire creation is structured with manifold types of conflicting opposites): the first of the opposites in Nature: Being as progression (*Spenta Mainyu*) will hold the secret of the entire universe. *Spenta Mainyu* (progression, fullness) and *Angra Mainyu* (regression, lack and estrangement) are always locked up in states of conflict.

It is through the meeting of these opposites that the universe is created. And yet though the meeting of the opposite forces create the entire cosmos, *Spenta Mainyu* as the solidness of "Being", is always somewhat stronger, and also has the upper hand over the nothingness of *Angra Mainyu*.

If Zarathushtra thus becomes a dialectician of Nature, he also becomes a philosopher of the human mind studying the regressive force as the dark aspect of the human mind. For *Angra Mainyu* is not merely the "lack" and estrangement, but almost a type of the repressed unconscious. As a dialectician of Nature he studies the Big Bang and the way progression (*Spenta Mainyu*) and regression (*Angra Maiyu*) work together. As a philosopher of the mind he studies human nature, especially the streak that humanity has for being seduced by the violence of *Angra Mainyu*. The conflict between *Spenta Mainyu* and *Angra Mainyu* is not only the conflict between light and darkness, but also the conflict between the conscious and the unconscious.

Yet Zarathushtra is also the prophet who promises that the end of this conflict will take place. He is the first of the prophets who says that the cessation of conflict is inevitable. Paradise lies thus at the end of Zarathushtra's conception of history. The Zoroastrians call this, as we already noted, Paradise: *Frašō-kereti* ("wonderful healing" and "renovation").

So if there is a beginning—a grand *Ur*-beginning—in Zoroastrianism, there is also the end. The beginning is the Big Bang with the dual forces in nature. The end is the negation of this struggle with the heralding of Paradise. Because of this structure of Zarathushtra's dialectic it would not be incorrect to call this logic *messianic teleology*, or even *messianic historicism*, driven by the clash of the two forces in the universe. There are, as if, two sorts of primal energies that are burning in the cosmos. But since Zarathushtra uses the words "*Mainyū*,"[99] it is best to translate it as "spirit" or "mind". Hegel's term *Geist* could be a better rendering. And yet when Zarathushtra recognizes these two forces, he also gives a normative understanding of them. One is good (*Vahyō*), while the other is evil (*Akem*).[100] From these two forces with their moral derivations, Zarathushtra says that wisdom, and the lack of wisdom, lie at the basis of the human condition. Here humanity is, as if, compelled to choose between these two primal forces. Thus there is the objective logic—good/bad and the subjective logic—wisdom/un-wisdom, with choice working as the groundwork of Zarathushtra's philosophy. So we have an objective logic, a subjective logic and a philosophy of action.

One thus begins with Zarathushtra's grand beginning (*pourye*)[101] structured with "the two paths" (*avarena*).[102] Humanity is almost compelled to decide on which of the pathways she or he decides to tread.[103] And since cosmic wisdom in the form of Mazda is said to be the creator of both these forces[104] there can be nothing that lies outside the Creator God. But this leads to the fundamental problem of evil—evil lies within God's own terrain. But then why does God, who is said to be omnipotent, omniscient and omnipresent, allow evil to exist?

Now those familiar with the teachings of the Gnostics know that there are two possibilities. The first claims that God is essentially good. But he is like a Greek tragic hero who seeing that his own creation is a blunder is unable to intervene and almost like Shakespeare's Hamlet feigns a sort of existential dilemma—"To be or not to be". The Zurvanists, according to Shahrastani, held the view that Ahriman arose from the doubt that Ohrmuzd had in his mind: *"What if there is someone equal to me?"* The other option is that God is not a tragic and doubting hero unable to rescue humanity from the onslaught of this mysterious force of evil. God here is some sort of sadomasochistic character who loves seeing his own creation suffer. But both these options do not apply for Zarathushtra's Ahura Mazda.

This gives rise to the fundamental philosophical problem—why does Mazda create evil? One has to answer this very fundamental problem. Since this issue was raised firstly by Zarathushtra in 1500 B.C.E. and then probably last stated emphatically in the ninth century C.E. Zoroastrian book of creative evolution, the *Bundahišn*, one will have to consider the historicity of this issue and the way the problem is posed and answered, as well as the continuity of the answers. For one thing, despite the different philosophical perspectives of the various Zoroastrian texts and non-Zoroastrian works (Greco, Roman and Islamic) the theme is constant. Evil is a domain that is diametrically opposite to goodness. These are so rigidly distinct that (as we mentioned) European scholars of Zoroastrianism have classified Zoroastrianism as a dualistic theology.[105] But the fact that the theme of the war of the two opposite forces that comprises the motor mechanism of the entire cosmic history ought to be classified as "dialectical" and not "dualist" did not occur to the European scholars for two fundamental ideological reasons: (1) In claiming that Zoroastrianism is dualist, it meant denigrating Ahura Mazda from the position of the Supreme Being to a co-principle accompanied also by the Evil One, and (2) Since the philosophy of Hegel is said to be dialectical and also since Marxism is the heir to the dialectical philosophy of Hegel, it is best to cut the impact of Zoroastrianism and at best read it as an ancient theology with no impact on modernity and also to forget the radical conclusions of Zarathushtra. But then how is one to move from the trap set by Orientalism?

Let us first move to Hegel's *Philosophy of History* who unlike mainstream history of philosophy brings in Zarathushtra and grants him the place of the first dialectician in history. To make matters easier by bringing Zarathushtra to the present, we move to Hegel's reading of Zoroastrianism (which he takes from Plutarch's rendering). Notice the war between the two opposing forces—*Ohrmuzd* (the Good One)—here Ahura Mazda has become *Ohrmuzd*—and *Ahriman* (the Zoroastrian Evil Force):

> There is not one Being (*Wesen*) which rules and guides the world, but good and evil are intermixed, or in short, nature produces nothing which is not combined with something else; so there is not a single dispenser who, like a barman, takes two flasks and pours out one drink mixed with another. On the contrary, what happens comes about through two opposed and antagonist principles, one of which directs us to the right, while the other pushes us to the opposite side. If not the whole universe, then at least this earth is moved in this unequal way. Zoroaster has presented this admirably by making one principle (Ohrmuzd) light and the other (Ahriman) darkness; midway between the two is Mithra called mediator by the Persians.
>
> Thus Mithra is also the substance, the universal Being, the sun, raised to the totality. He is not the mediator between Ohrmuzd and Ahriman in the sense of being a peacemaker, in which case both of them would remain subsisting independently; on the contrary, he is on Ohrmuzd's side and fights along with him against the evil principle. Mithra does not participate in good and evil nor is he an unholy thing in the centre between them.
>
> Ahriman is sometimes called the first-born son on light, but Ohrmuzd has alone remained in the light. At the creation of the visible world Ohrmuzd set upon the earth, into his incomprehensible kingdom of light, the fixed vault of heaven which is above all and yet is surrounded everywhere by the first original light. In the middle of the earth is the

high mountain Albordi which rises in the original light. Ohrmuzd's realm of light lies undisturbed above the fixed vault of heaven and all along Albordi, and therefore on the earth too until the third age. At that point Ahriman, whose realm of night was previously bound beneath the earth, broke in upon in upon Ohrmuzd's corporeal world and ruled in common with him. The space between heaven and earth is now halved into day and night. Just as Ohrmuzd previously had only one spiritual realm of light, so Ahriman had only one night; but now having forced his way in, Ahriman opposed a terrestrial creation of night into the terrestrial creation of light. From now on, two corporeal worlds stand over against one another, one pure and good, the other impure and evil. This opposition runs through the whole of nature. On Albordi Ohrmuzd created Mithra as mediator for the earth. The aim of the creation of the terrestrial world is none other than by its means to restore the beings who had fallen away from their creator, to make them good again, and to make evil disappear forever. The terrestrial world is the seat and the ground of the battle between good and evil; but the battle between light and darkness is not an absolutely and inherently unresolved opposition, but a transient one. Ohrmuzd, the principle of light will conquer.[106]

But there is another modern and philosophical rendering of Zoroastrianism—that of Friedrich Nietzsche:

Zarathustra was the first to see in the struggle between good and evil the actual wheel in the working of things: the translation of morality into the realm of metaphysics, as force, cause, end-in-itself, in *his* work. But this question is itself at bottom its own answer. Zarathustra *created* the most fateful of all errors, morality: consequently he must also be the first to *recognize* it. Not only has he had longer and greater experience here than any other thinker—the whole of history is indeed the experimental refutation of the proposition of the so-called 'moral order'—what is more important is that Zarathustra is more truthful than any other thinker. His teaching, and his alone, upholds truthfulness as the supreme virtue—that is to say, the opposite of the *cowardice* of the 'idealist', who takes flight in the face of reality; Zarathustra has more courage in

> him than all the thinkers put together. To tell the truth and *to shoot well with arrows*: that is the Persian virtue—Have I been understood? The self-overcoming of morality through truthfulness, the self-overcoming of the moralist into his opposite—into me—that is what the name Zarathustra means in my mouth.[107]

Zarathushtra and the Question of Secular-Humanism

Since secularism seems to be an unresolved part in Iranian history and since Zarathustra's name now appears more often than not, usually in the spaces left vacant by Stalinism in Eastern Europe, neoliberalism in the West and messianic Shiiteism in Iran, one needs both to understand these processes as also to listen to what Edward Said who once said:

> The major influences on George W. Bush's Pentagon and National Security Council were men such as Bernard Lewis and Fouad Ajami, experts on the Arab and Islamic world who helped the American hawks to think about such preposterous phenomena as the Arab mind and centuries-old Islamic decline which only American power could reverse. Today bookstores in the US are filled with shabby screeds bearing screaming headlines about Islam and terror, Islam exposed, the Arab threat and the Muslim menace, all of them written by political polemicists pretending to knowledge imparted to them and others by experts who have supposedly penetrated to the heart of these strange Oriental peoples. Accompanying such war-mongering expertise have been CNN and Fox, plus myriad evangelical and right-wing radio hosts, innumerable tabloids and even middle-brow journals, all of them re-cycling the same unverifiable fictions and vast generalizations so as to stir up "America" against the foreign devil.[108]

Not only does Zarathushtra's name occur in Iran, this theme of the return of Zoroastrianism in Tajikistan is also often heard. In 2006 President Rahmonov declared that Tajikistan celebrate its "Aryan" civilization reminding the people and the world of their "glorious past" and showing how they can once again build a "glorious future". The fact that the failure of

Stalinism, messianic theology and neoliberalism stands behind the quest for born-again Zoroastrianism ought to be stressed.

While the dictatorship of the mullahs in Iran did (and yet does) obliterate Iranian national identity (many to feel that they are non-Muslim), one must also note that the Kurds in Iran had approached the Imperial Court of the Shah of Iran to be included as Zoroastrians.[109] Philip Kreyenbroek also includes the Yezidis and the Al Haqqs as belonging to a subaltern Zoroastrian sect,[110] though externally they seem to be Muslim. In India there is a Zoroastrian group called the *Ilm-e-Khshnoom,* rallying around Meher Master Moos which has connections with the people of Tajikistan who claim to be Zoroastrian. Besides the Tajikis (they have named their Press Trust, *Avesta,* following the Holy Book of the Zoroastrians), it is also the people of Uzbekistan who claim to be of Zoroastrian descent.[111] Besides identity politics in West Asia it must also be noted that the most celebrated of the neo-Zoroastrians is the Swedish philosopher and musician, Alexander Bard who places Zarathushtra as a philosopher at par with Spinoza, Nietzsche and Deluze, while the first American "convert" (to the horror of the orthodox Parsi priests) was Richard Peterson.

Keeping these very important themes of identity politics (excluding both Bard and Peterson) bound also in the last resort to the politics of imperialism, the makings of the Empire and Asian studies, one states that studies in Zoroastrianism are important not merely for understanding the history of Iran from the Indo-Iranian migrations to the construction of the Oriental state, the foundations of both world philosophy and monotheism, the problem of human freedom formulated in the ancient world, along with the problems of the theocratic state invented by Sasanian Zoroastrianism. For understanding these important facets of Zoroastrianism, one goes back to Iran and understands the pathways that link the civilizations of the Greeks, the Romans, the Iranian, the Babylonians, the Chinese and the Indians. That Shiite Islam is philosophically and historically a combination of Zoroastrianism and Islam, just as Zoroastrianism is linked to Judaism and Christianity, on the one hand, and Hinduism and Buddhism, on the other hand, is something which conservatism in religious studies yet does not recognize. That the ruling right-wing elite of Iran deny both the imperial Zoroastrianism, as well as the Gnostic-Zoroastrian and Mazdakite foundations of Shiite Islam is probably one of the single biggest cultural crises emerging in Iran. Iran's bridging the dialogue between the East and the West that ought to facilitate the great dialogue of civilizations seems to be closed. The fault lies in the pre-secular world of the Asiatic mode of production, the institution of religion as the weapon of the ruling classes and the hegemony of the various "Churches": the Zoroastrian, Christian and the Islamic. But then the fault lies also with messianic ideology itself. For no messianic ideology is comfortable in allowing other messianic ideologies in its own fold. Sasanian Zoroastrianism did not allow Mani (in fact executed him and exiled his followers), just as it did not allow Mazdak (and executed him too). The seeds of the destruction of Zoroastrianism were sown in its own Oriental Despotic cranium. The tradition of Oriental Despotism still continues. The crown of Ardashīr Papakan is now worn by the Iranian Ayatollahs. Though historians, Mary Boyce is an example, have insisted on the civilizational conflict between Muslims and the Zoroastrians in Iran (a point that one will have to severely disagree with), the modern Zoroastrians in Muslim countries have an existence that is wholly different than the one portrayed by the Orientalists. Consider what Ayub Khan the late President of Pakistan had to say about the Zoroastrians in Pakistan:

> The teachings of the prophet Zoroaster are indeed, a source of infinite inspiration not only to the Parsees but to all those who believe in the sanctity of moral and spiritual values in human lives. It redounds to the credit of the Parsee community that they have endeavoured to translate the teachings of their prophet to their day to day lives and have sought to apply the principles of their religion to the practical fields of social and economic enterprise. Pakistan has every reason to be proud of her Parsee citizens who have contributed so much to the progress and development of the nation. Spirit of loyalty and unreserved co-operation which the Parsees have shown

> wherever they have settled down is a tribute to the greatness of their religion as to their wisdom. The people of Karachi owe a great debt of gratitude to the Parsee community for the immense contribution they have made to the economic development of the city. The many welfare institutions which the Parsee philanthropists have raised in Karachi are a boon to its citizens. The tradition of public welfare which Parsees have built is worthy of emulation by other communities in Karachi and elsewhere in Pakistan....It will be our earnest endeavour to ensure that Parsees—like other communities—continue to enjoy equal rights as free citizens of a free country. You have rightly observed the patriotism of the Parsees is second to none. Nobody is more conscious than I of the great patriotic zeal which you have displayed. [112]

Amongst the Pakistani Parsis the following names come up—the author Bapsi Sidhwa, Justice Dorab Patel (1927-1997), one of the judges in the trial of Bhutto and the only one who delivered the judgement that the hanging of Bhutto was wrong,[113] while other successful Pakistani Parsis have been Brigadier F. Golwalla and Colonel Sarosh Irani (both decorated in the 1965 Indo-Pakistan war) and more recently Major General Kaizad Sopariwalla.[114] Just as the Parsis were prominent in the making of modern Bombay, so were the Parsis in the making of Karachi.

At least in modern imagination the Parsi as the patriot (be it the Indian or the Pakistani Parsi) is imprinted. So far there has been no satisfactory explanation as to why this "goodness" prevails even in popular imagination. One possible explanation is that they are not seen to be threatening and thus classified as "good" and "patriotic". The better explanation is that they have taken the role of the liberal bourgeoisie with their welfare measures, thus letting the "goodness" and "patriotism" have material effects. One will have to point out that the site of dualism functioning in modern capitalist societies (that of the clash between the private and public realms, the religious and the secular identities that Marx so eloquently pointed out in *On the Jewish Question*) is absent in the Parsis.[115] The Parsis are comfortably Parsi and Indian, Pakistani, Iranian, American, etc.

Moving from the idea of modernity and secularism and proceeding into the domain of the messiahs, it must be noted that the idea of the Missing Imam is also a Zoroastrian invention. A close look at the political discourse of the contemporary Islamic regime in Iran will notice echoes of Zoroastrianism. For Zoroastrianism, the virtuous "truth tellers" hasten the advent of the Saoshyant, or the promised future messiah. It must also be noted that it was Zoroastrianism which invented the ideas of the End of History, the Last Day, the Resurrection of the Dead, and Eternal Afterlife, ideas that are fundamental not only for Shiite Iran, but also for Judaism and Christianity. If one notes Ahmadinejad's ideology mimics the old Zoroastrian ideology of the war between good and evil. For Ahmadinejad, Iran is good while the USA is afflicted with the disease given by Ahriman. Even the contemporary Iranian regime's recalling of Imam Mahdi to fight Zionist Israel and the USA is a clear recalling of the idea of the Zoroastrian saviour.

And yet it must also be noted that the messianic question of what Walter Benjamin called *the blowing up of the continuum of history*[116] cannot be given to two messianic traditions. One messianic tradition has to give way to another. Messianic historicism thus operates as some sort of a bad-Hegelianism where the messianic *Auhfebung* (transcendence, abolition, preservation) is said to sublate the truth of *all* reality in its own cranium. The messianic cranium becomes the theological Absolute Idea where nothing can exist except its own narcissistic self. One simply has to accept the messiah so as not to fall into error, or worse still, simply commit heresy. Even today disbelief in God in theological Iran is stated as enmity with God (*moharebeh*) and punishable by death. After the 1979 anti-communist counterrevolution, when the Iranian mullahs began re-inventing their brand of Islam, the history of Iran (prior to 1979) was classified as *jahiliyyah*, or the "Dark Age". It must be noted that in the early days of the counterrevolution, the Islamic counterrevolutionaries tried to destroy Persepolis. Cyrus was said to be a sodomite Jew and attempts have been made to erase all memories of Zoroastrian historiography. The result has been exactly the opposite. As has recently been said:

> The Persian language, spoken by a majority of Iran's multiethnic society, and long considered a bastion of Iranian nationalism, has not been immune from the vicissitudes of this culture war either. While much was made of cleansing the Persian language of any Arabic words and influence during the Pahlavi era, Ayatollah Khomeini and his allies made an equally concentrated and futile attempt to infuse the language with more and more Arabic words, phrases and even grammatical structures. For them, Arabic is the language of God and of the *Koran*, while to the Iranian nationalists it is a detested tool of Arab and Islamic cultural invasion. Just as the effort to create a new "Islamic society" has failed, the attempt to introduce Arabic into the Persian language has also been unsuccessful. Not only is the Persian vernacular today replete with new, cleverly constructed Persian words, but a whole generation of parents are increasingly moving away from naming their children after religious figures, opting instead for names from Iran's mytho-history, or newly minted names conjured or coined from the Persian vocabulary. In this sense, then, the 1979 revolution was only a moment in the centuries-old culture war to define the soul of Iran; yet another attempt in the long line of efforts to eliminate or diminish in influence certain components of the country's bifurcated identity.[117]

Now there is another problem that messianic historicism has led to: the de-linking of not only Iran from its Persian foundations, but also the de-linking of Western philosophy from the culture of Iran, thus deforming also the processes of modernity and secularism in Iran. The single biggest burden that Iran carries even today is the inability of Iran to openly secularize itself. What is called the *Öffentlichkeit*, or the public space, even the open space, is simply not possible in Iran with the dictatorship of the transcendental and missing messiahs. If Iranian politics modernizes itself, then it is only at the level of societal modernization, which it in fact borrows from the crisis-ridden technological reason and the instrumental rationality of West European and North American capitalism. Islamic Iran today simply cannot culturally modernize itself. The messiah is no modernist.

It is these historical gaps that one needs filling, whereby one is able to replace the clash of civilizations thesis with the clash of economic modes and the even bigger clash of the messiahs. For if Zarathushtra is known to the world as the prophet of ancient Iran, whose teachings of God's conflict with the forces of evil; there is also another Zarathushtra, known to the world—the Zarathushtra who apparently has not yet landed in Iran—the Zarathustra of Nietzsche, the apocalyptic nihilist of the romantic anti-capitalist genre, who announces the death of God. Hitherto there is no philosophical tract comparing these two Zarathushtras. R.C. Zaehner had almost debunked the Nietzschean Zarathustra.[118] While the first remains a part of Zoroastrian legend, the second becomes a part of Western philosophy. The Zarathustra of Nietzsche who comes out from the solitude of the mountains to go and give the message of the *Ubermensch* (the overman) was taken up by Martin Heidegger, Michel Foucault, Gilles Deleuze and Jacques Derrida.

That the two Zarathushtras meet, at least philosophically—one that announces the birth of God, the other the death—is something that the two philosophical traditions (the Persian and the Western philosophical one) have hitherto never tried reconciling. But despite Nietzsche's anarcho-syndicalist rendering of Zarathushtra, Zoroastrianism is best known to the world as the religious-ideology of the Persians who flee to India to keep alive the memory of their messiah. "Remembrance" becomes a remembrance in exile. Now the flight of the Zoroastrians to India is not much known either to the world at large or to the academic community. It is said that the attack on Iran was an essential part of the cosmic drama of the conflict between good and evil. The late sixteenth century C.E. text, the *Qessa-ye-Sanjan* or the *Kisseh-e-Sanjan* ("The Story of Sanjan"), mentions how thrice the tyrant will appear and shatter the religion of Zarathushtra.[119]

There are two different pathways opened: (1) the secular and rational pathway followed by the modern Parsis who do not lament the "fall" from legendary grace (and most of all more then the critique of Islam as the new religious ideology in dominance in Iran, critique the Sasanian state), and (2) the path which criticizes apocalyptic Shiite Islam as the root of all problems in Iran.

In contrast to both these views is the view held by the Worker-Communist Party of Iran which states that political Islam as the dominant ideology of the state of Iran is due to the crisis of global capitalism, where political-apocalyptic Islam is helped by the imperialist powers to manage late imperialism in permanent crisis. Maryam Namazie (member of the Worker-Communist Party of Iran), for instance, talks of how the leftists "have suffered at the hands of Islam", because they suffer at the hands of global capitalism, imperialism and anti-left governments. After all, it is well known that the present theological government of Iran "protects" the rights of the Zoroastrians, the Jews and the Christians as the "people of the Book". It is the masses at large, along with democratic forces fighting the right-wing government that have had to suffer under theological regimes. Most importantly, political Islam (like political theology in general) is the best tool for crisis-ridden imperialism and is a necessary part of the geo-politics of global capital accumulation. To put an alleged "violent" Islamic Iran as against an "innocent" Christian West (as also an "evil" Islam as against a "good" Zoroastrianism) is thus a part of the management of global capitalism. After all it has never been asked: "*Why (do) the ideologists turn everything upside down* (*auf den Koph stellen*)?"[120] And why has one not been asked the question: Why is political theology the "general expression" (*Ausdruck*) of the dominant class whose general function is *repression*?[121] Asking these very real questions can wake us up from the dreams of the romantic inventions of "Golden Ages" and the seekers of "traditions."

And yet since identities are continuously manufactured, and since the contemporary Iranian regime actively denies the possibilities of evolving into a secular state, there is the feeling that is aroused by the pan-Iranian movement in contemporary Iran: Why not try Zoroastrianism as the cultural politics of Iran? Could national memory be activated, after all, the pan-Iranist in Iran asks: Was Islam not forced in the last resort onto the Iranian masses? And the same pan-Iranist asks even now:

Is not the cultural memory of Zoroastrianism present in the masses of Iran? Would the case of Firdausi's *Sháhanáma* not be sufficient to illustrate the point that the Iranian memory is primarily *Iranian* and tempered in the deep structure by Zarathushtra's teachings of the embracement of Life and that this *Lebensphilosophie* cannot be suppressed by the politics of denial and state-sponsored repression? Maybe (so the pan-Iranist in Iran asks) there can be a forgetfulness of history, but memories can always be activated. Perhaps then this great Iranian tragedy will be over. A Soviet anthology in tune with this line of thinking had recalled the Azerbaijani writer Mirza Fatali Akhundov's lament:

> O, Iranian people! If only you had tasted the sweetness of freedom, if only you had versed in the rights of mankind, you would never had consented to such a shameful enslavement and to submissiveness.....Your numbers and resources are a hundred times greater than those of the despots and the tyrants; you lack only the unity of thought and spirit to forge a revolution and free yourself from slavery.[122]

The same anthology contrasts the folk art of Azerbaijan to "the lifeless dogma of Islam and religious bigotry".[123] It also traces its folk history to its ancient folk name "Odlar Yurdu" (the Land of Fires) and "Sheir Yurdu" (the Land of Poetry).[124] That fire has been part of the poetic metaphor of all the Iranian people has not to be missed out. Remember Zarathushtra, like Prometheus, seizes the fire from the gods and gives it to humanity. And just as Zarathushtra, in order to achieve Paradise, was *successful in the ordeal through fire,*[125] so too the Iranian people have to go through the brook of fire in order to be emancipated. That Zarathushtra's name crops up repeatedly in what was once Eastern Iran is no surprise. We mentioned earlier, that today the Tajik Press calls itself the "Avesta". But then traditions like communities are continuously imagined. And if one lives in the realm of what Benedict Anderson calls "imagined communities", the Lacanian Imaginary displaces the Real, and constructs the phantasmagoria that humanity is primarily religious and that traditions are likewise religious traditions.

The recalling of the thinker from antiquity, who is said to have first taught the doctrine of human freedom, becomes centrally important. And because Iran not only denies its own philosopher who preached about freedom, but primarily denies its own freedom; and also because its own understanding of messianic eschatology has gone wrong; the spectre of Zarathushtra emerges again. Like Marx's spectre of communism which is most certainly haunting all Europe (if not the whole world): "A spectre is haunting Europe—the spectre of communism" (*Ein Gespenst geht um in Europa—das Gespenst des Kommunismus*)[126]; the spectre of Zarathushtra it seems (despite it being driven away by the theologians) is again haunting all Iran. And if it is not haunting Iran, it is being made to haunt Iran. Yet, it must be noted, Zarathushtra is only a metaphor for "Persianness" that the secular masses of Iran are crying for. More than the figure of Zarathushtra, it is the memory of Cyrus that is evoked. To recall Milani again:

> And within this paradigm was forged the uneasy relationship with the West still present in the battle to reconcile Iranian identity—particularly the pre-Islamic elements—with Enlightenment values. It may be masked beneath the heavy shroud of the current theocratic regime, but it lies in wait. Montesquieu might well have been the first to recognize the inherent difficulties of this sort of resolution when, in his *Persian Letters*, he asked how one can be at once modern and Persian. Indeed, among the advocates of a democratic polity—no less influential but far less famous—were the often self-effacing scholars, poets, historians, writers and musicians who in those years worked hard to discover, preserve, publish and display critical, often-ignored elements of Iran's imperial era as well as its post-Islamic cultural heritage. Their efforts were indispensable to the emergence of a new form of Iranian cultural modernity that was less awed and intimidated by the West and more inclined to infuse into their work usable elements of Iran's own tradition. From music and architecture to painting and poetry, there was initially a rush to reproduce in Iran the styles and forms that were popular in the West. But by the late sixties and early seventies, something fundamental happened to many advocates of this Westophile modernity;

they forsook their earlier attempts at simply imitating the works of Western masters and began an eventful age of the "return" to native roots. Transcending the tradition of old and incorporating it into the best the West had to offer, rather than simply emulating the Western way of life, became the motto of this new Iranian ethos. Many cultural fields witnessed this profound process of looking inward while innovating.[127]

But turning to traditions, or even searching for alleged *"civilizational roots"*, can become more problematic than ever. On the one hand, one can have a historical understanding of civilizations that understands diverse cultures with retrospective to their economic modes of production and the historical conjuncture of class struggles. On the other hand, there is the romantic tradition of looking at civilizational *"foundations"*. In this romantic *looking back,* one becomes like Benjamin's angel of history looking backwards despite being blown forward by the great storm of progress.[128] And beneath the angel, as Benjamin rightly notes, are ruins

So looking for traditions could be a dangerous affair. It is well known that the second Shah of twentieth century Iran, Shah Reza Pahalvi, thought of tracing his roots directly to Cyrus the Great. That the end result of this searching of roots was the 1979 Islamic counterrevolution and the rule of the dictatorship of the fundamentalist theologians ought not to go unrecognized. That *Tawhidi* or political Islam in Iran (which even once seduced Michel Foucault who in his *What are the Iranians Dreaming Of?* celebrated the mullah-state nexus) which excludes the process of humanization and instead gives consent to the politics of the committee of the clerics (*Velayat-e Faqif*), one need not turn to the *Koran* but to real history and (as we already pointed out) to the first Sasanian monarch Papakan who in his doctrine of the brotherhood between religion and kingship had institutionalized state theology in Iran.[129] Considering that this was true, it is strange, because for the historical Zarathushtra, such a view was anathema for him. So what was anathema for Zarathushtra became a part of the doctrine of his followers, as well as the enemy of the followers. In this case, *Tawhidi* Islam learns more from the Oriental state of Iran than its own Prophet Muhammad. The crisis emerging in Iran is the crisis of the world bourgeois order accompanied by the crisis of the anti-modernists in Iran. They can never directly answer the question: Is the individual an autonomous being, free from the control of the state and from the fear of the fetishism of the wrathful God who regularly creates havoc?

That searching for traditions is nothing but, what Marx calls, "making the ghost walk about again" speaking in "borrowed language" and "borrowed speech" and wandering aimlessly like "shadows that have lost their bodies"[130] has also to be noted. Authenticity, on the other hand, searches for the humanist understanding of history, a search where a universal understanding of humanity can be explored. The project of understanding civilizations makes sense in this humanist and class-based subaltern perspective of historical materialism. It was Samir Amin who had said that there are three waves of the emergences of the *humanist concept of universalism* and the *universalist concept of humanity*: the first wave starting with Zarathushtra, that includes Judaism, Buddhism, Hellenism, Confucianism, Christianity and culminating with the teachings of Muhammad. The second wave is of the European Enlightenment that culminated in the French Revolution (Amin should have included the Sufis), while the third wave is of Marxism and the establishment of an international classless world order.[131] It is in the large space where one understands different perspectives of the flowering of humanism and internationalism and the dialogue between civilizations such that a rational understanding of the human past can be decoded.

It was said sometime in the last century that Zarathushtra too carried his sword like Muhammad,[132] and that Zarathushtra was "the prophet of lightning."[133] So do we have one more Zarathushtra—a sword-wielding prophet? Are the builders of great Utopias also necessarily the destroyers of civilizations? Or are they destroyers of class-based civilizations who follow the German bard's line of thinking: "for all that comes to birth, is fit for overthrow as nothing as nothing worth?"[134]

Did Zarathushtra preach not only with the weapons of criticism, but also with the weapon itself? But elsewhere the same thinker who thought that Zarathushtra carried a sword says that the Zoroastrian God is not wrathful,[135] in fact denies wrath and with it the carrying of weapons. Zarathushtra cannot bear weapons. The "good word" of Zarathushtra turns into the criticism of weapons. Yet we find if not the prophets, then at least those who carry forth their names, the bearers of weapons, weapons that are directed against the population at large. How is this possible?

There is one rendering of the weapon-bearing messiahs. Marx's observations that people have lost their human essence (*das menschliche Wesen*), and in doing so are smoking the phantasmagorical pipe of the opium of religion[136] comes to mind. But then it is also said that religion, even in its totemic-fantastic and duplicated form, cannot simply be overcome. The *Aufhebung* of religion is then said to be impossible. According to this liberal rendering, the best form of religion is an international consensus based religion that understands how diverse religions can exist in a pluralist, international democratic order.

So how does one rescue religion from the religious fundamentalist? Now it is known (and argued not only by the Muslim liberal, but actively propagated by the *Ilm-e-Khshnoom*, a Zoroastrian "mystical" sect in India) that Islam's prophet had said that, "every people hath its apostle,"[137] and Islam cannot be hegemonic and the destroyer of civilizations. The same Zoroastrian sect calls Muhammad the return of Zarathushtra, though this is in direct contrast to all possible Zoroastrian and Islamic literature.

The main fault of the idealist conception of history (which incorporates the philosophy of the messiah) and manifests itself as Orientalism is the inability to understand political economy and history. That Islam is called a "Mohammedean revolution"[138] whose aim was to establish "the principle of "no property in land" throughout the whole of Asia"[139] has to be understood. Whether there was real interaction between the communist Mazdakites and Muhammad and whether the *Koran* absorbed Mazdakite ideas is yet unclear. But that Salman Farsi was to some extent providing information on Iran to the prophet of Islam as also Muhammad's (as also the Arabs') knowledge of Iran and its culture is most certainly known. This is the main binding thread—the class struggles in Sasanian Iran and the place of the Arabs in the Sasanian Empire. The rest is all derivative. After all, one knows that invasion and occupation have been part of human history and Islam is at no fault. Trying to blame Islam for invasions and the consequent collapse of Zoroastrianism is historically incorrect. What Muhammad did was firstly to perfect the ideology of the awakening of Arabic national consciousness and then to lead them to unification. Islam did not invent the wars against Iran. Remember that the Arabs were broken into three kingdoms one of which (the buffer Lakhmid state) was run over by the forces of Khausrau II. The Sasanians used to displace all rebellious populations since the times Shapur II and the displacement of the Arabs was no exception.

Instead the Arabic internal tribal wars and then the two brief but swift wars with Iran have to be seen in the perspective of the collapse of Arabic trade, the destruction of their cities and the imperial policies of Iran and Rome. After all, force (especially revolutionary seizure of power), to borrow Marx's phrase, "is the midwife of every society pregnant with a new one. It is itself an economic power."[140] The mega cities of the ancient world were breaking up. The gap between town and country was becoming too vast. Just as Ancient Rome was attacked by the neighbouring tribes, so too the Arabs were running over the Sasanian Empire. But with the deaths of Muhammad and Ali, the green flag of the Muslim revolution was lowered. Mu'awiyah and Yazid (the assassins of the Muslim revolutionaries) and the new Muslim elites would be the first to see that the class order was restored. Instead of the revolutionary kernel of Islamic teachings, it was only the shell that was being propagated. That is of course till Jalal-u-Din Rumi and the Persian Sufis came along. This is how the actual landscape looked like. In this landscape one finds neither purely Zoroastrianism, nor a "pure" Islam, but quite something else:

> The absence of private property in land is indeed the key to the whole of the East. Herein lies its political and religious history. But how does it come about that the Orientals have not arrived at landed property, even in its feudal form? I think it is mainly due to climate, taken in connection with the nature of the soil, especially with the great stretches of desert which extended from the Sahara straight across Arabia, Persia, India and Tatary up to the highest Asiatic plateau. Artificial irrigation is here the first condition of agriculture and this is a matter either for the communes, the provinces or the central government. An Oriental government never had more than three departments: finance (plunder at home), war (plunder at home and abroad) and public works (provision at home and abroad).[141]

It is in this space—that is neither Zoroastrian, nor Islamic—that one understands the further (post-Sasanian) history that talks of how "Arabs, Turks, Tartars, Mughals who had successfully overrun India, soon became *Hinduized*, the barbarian conquers being, by the eternal law of history, conquered by the superior civilization of those subjects."[142] But then, one will have to argue from the Zoroastrian point of view, even though one knows of the synthesis taking place between Zoroastrianism and Islam, did this "eternal law of history" work in Iran, whereby a superior civilization that was subjugated militarily able to culturally overwhelm the invaders? Or did Zoroastrianism in proclaiming that the world saviour will come, then fade away when the saviour did indeed appear?

To preclude any construction of Islamophobia one needs to mention a subaltern and materialist reading of history. What we now know (and this is what has recently been pointed out by Peter Hudis) that European rationalism was directly influenced by al-Farabi, Ibn Sina, and Averroes, that Descartes was inspired by al-Ghazzali, and that al-Sijistani influenced dialectical thinking.[143] One should also not forget

Hegel's reference to the Sufi mystic Rumi in his *Phenomenology of Mind.*[144]

In contrast to this radical materialist reading of history one gets another theoretical problematic. A contemporary compendium on Zoroastrianism, that proudly decks many Zoroastrian homes in India, mentions how the footprints of Zoroastrianism are yet found in the present Kurds, Yezidis, Ahl-e-Haq, even the Shiites; besides allegedly influencing in the past Judaism, Northern Buddhism, Christianity and Islam.[145] But in the last resort, even in the narrative of the grand influences, Zoroastrianism almost disappears from the face of the earth, Like the ancient Zoroastrian myth of creation, Gayômart—literally "the first mortal", or at least the first proto-human—the father of the human race in dying, in a libidinal state of ecstasy, scatters his seeds, and in doing so gives birth to the first couple, Masya and Masyani[146]; so too Zoroastrianism in giving birth has to die. Zoroastrianism, as Nietzsche's dictum went: *dies at the right time.*[147] But at least one child that it gave birth to decides to kill the parent. So why did Zoroastrianism have to die? Let us have a look at the Zoroastrian myth again. Ahriman, the Iranian devil wants to destroy the good earth. But because the good creation is protected by Ohrmuzd, the principle of eternal goodness and light (the rendering of the Zoroastrian God (Ahura Mazda) himself), Ahriman is unsuccessful till he sends Jahî, the Primal Whore and his consort to seduce Gayômart (the "first man" or the "Iranian Adam").[148] Note how in this narrative class societies open the way for the discourses of patriarchy. Gayômart is destroyed by lust, or at least surplus lust, not to forget class civilization's oldest enemy, the woman embodied as the feminine principle of the "eternal whore". Just as Ahriman, the principle of wrath, stupidity and destruction (with the help of the woman) has attacked the good earth, so now the Arabs have attacked the good nation of Iran. What is left is only memory. Resistance is expressed in the apocalyptic book of creation, where the destruction of the Arabs is foretold firstly by a community of red ensigns and red banners, (the author seems to be referring to the communist Mazdakites operating under the probable name of "Muhammira"[149]) followed by the Turks and the Romans, culminating in the return of the glory (*Khvareh*) of the royal family of Iran which will rule over Hindustan, Rome and Turkestan, where only the faith of Zarathushtra will prevail.[150] In contrast to this rather fantastic legend-making, a Persian poem (more in tune with the realism of the times) suggests only frozen memory:

> As the world will not remain constant to any,
> It is better that his goodness remains in memory.
> The world is permanent memory and we are to go.
> Nothing remains unto man save humanity.
> Commit not sin, o Sahâyar! So long as thou cast
> A sin-owing to which the soul may feel ashamed.
> Choose harmlessness and benevolence
> And this is the teaching and writing of the religion.[151]

There is another legend. This time the Zoroastrians enter India which is not only the land of the demonical *devas*, but also the land of what the *Avesta* calls, "abnormal menstruation…(and) the abnormal heat."[152] Now they do not wish to destroy the *devas*. On the contrary, it is passion to survive that brings them to India. They ask the chieftain, a certain Jadi Rana, according to Zoroastrian legend, for refuge. The Rana, fearful that the Persians might subdue his people, gives a glass of milk filled to the brim, suggesting that his land is already full, and the entry of the Persians, could upset the balance of forces. The leader of the Zoroastrians, then puts a pinch of sugar in the milk, signifying that they will not disturb the peace, only sweeten the land they seek to adopt as their own. An older dogma to destroy the *devas* was forgotten. After all when one moves from a position of hegemony to periphery then ideology too changes. From henceforth memory takes a different form. Besides the Persians are asked to give up their mother tongue and adopt the local language, Gujaṛati.[153] If language is the *House of Memories*, if not memories, then at least the language of memories would have to change.

But more than the discourse of milk and sugar signifying a new passion for survival and a new cultural exchange, it is the law of equal exchange—the driving force of civilizations—which helps not only the Zoroastrians survive in India, but thrive. The exchange between milk and sugar (rather commodity 'A' and commodity 'B') was, on the one hand, a symbolic gesture of peace and goodwill. On the other hand, it was the reliving of the probable most ancient act of human history—the exchange of commodities. And as usually told by the Marxists, this most ancient act, is the secret of our modern civilization—the creation of surplus value and economic wealth. The Zoroastrians, or at least, the Zoroastrians who came to India knew this. *Spenta Mainyu* would not be a mere theological term for them, but as signifying bountifulness, would imply the creation of material wealth. The spectre of the Arab invader would be exorcized.

But in Iran neither rational exchange nor the discourse of the manufacture of memories was simply so smooth going as for their brethren in India. And vulgar political economy or simply theft of property would initiate the process of their marginalization and ghettoization. The Zoroastrians would now be relegated down the social order of things. They would henceforth be *Gavra*, heretics, even *Najis*, unclean. The myth of the destruction of the religion of Zarathushtra would indeed be realized.[154]

The book of creation also mentions this *catastrophe*, and again, in *mythical* terms, where more than Zarathushtra's own praxical oriented humanist philosophy, we have the myth of conflicting nations (Iran vs. the Arabs) and the mystical time-cycle of the apocalyptic millennium dominating the text. That the damnation of the mythical "other" persists in this apocalyptic text has not to be forgotten. The Arabs are seen both in nationalist and religious terms. With the damnation of the "other", they are said to belong to a bad creed. They are said to do bizarre things like eating dead matter. There could be no worse calamity that has come to Iran.[155] *Orthodoxy* has now vanished from Iran along with *reason*, and the populace at large has no memory left of their national and religious identity.[156] The finger of accusation points to "evil-times" (a definite manifestation of the doctrine of the Zurvanists, where

Zurvan or Time was made out to be the principal actor of history, sometimes as is indeed said that *Zurvan* is the father of even God). The nobles and the upholders of religion are also said to have joined hands with the invaders. Those who wanted to learn the science of Zarathushtra, even in secret, had to do so with great pain, trouble and difficulty.[157] The invaders—the "brood of the Tâjís"[158]—remind the Zoroastrian imagination of Alexander (here called "the Roman").[159] And they (the Arabs) get the same place reserved for Alexander, they are the "accursed", a term mainly reserved for Ahriman the devil. They propagate only ill-will.[160]

But then why did a civilization who were taught, "to tell the truth and *to shoot well with arrows*,"[161] shift to the other side, the side of occupation and the colonization of the Iranian mind? And how does critique search for the conditions of the possibilities of secular humanism from within historical traditions?

Two points emerge with the seeking of traditions: the one used by Marx: "The tradition of all the dead generations weigh like a nightmare on the brains of the living,"[162] that seeking traditions is self-defeating, and if one form of hegemony is overcome then, another one (probably the monarchical one), will return. But there is also another modern rendering of tradition: the one used by Jürgen Habermas where traditions are not necessarily understood as the dead weight of a feudal or authoritarian past. Instead by traditions, here one implies life-worlds and the *historical embedding* of culture, what critical theory calls "the public use of tradition" and appropriating a "particular life-context anchored in the particular cultural form of life."[163]

For Iran one form of reliving tradition is realized only when the other one is eliminated. And to seek these traditions, both the burdensome as well as the not so troublesome traditions, one has now to leave the real Zarathushtra for the moment and go along Nietzsche's Zarathustra into the underworld. In fact the discourse of loss, memory and recovery is constituted in Zarathushtra's descent into the underworld.[164] But like

Nietzsche's Zarathushtra, the Zarathushtra of the Zoroastrians is laughing, even in the underworld.

Zarathushtra was, as we noted, born laughing. Laughter is almost as sort of a "philosophical discourse" even of the present Zoroastrians. Today not more than a hundred and fifty thousand followers remain, mostly settled in India. State-sponsored persecution in Iran has taught the Zoroastrians many things. One is to keep their religion to themselves and practise it only in the private domain. Yet wherever you may find them, one will find them laughing. The theme of laughter remains central for the Zoroastrians—joy they say is the way of Ahura Mazda, while despair is the cunning way of Ahriman the devil. Yet the story of Zoroastrianism has been a form of a tragedy far more subtle than the Greek or the Shakespearean ones. Post-651 C.E., has been a sort of a "fall" from grace where "the cunning of reason" (*die List der Vernunft*) as Hegel called it, took centre stage in Iranian history.

Zarathushtra in the Underworld

We noted before that according to Nietzsche's *Also sprach Zarathustra*, Zarathushtra (who is according to Parsi legend "the herald of the Golden Dawn" and "he of the Golden Light") has like the sun (from whom he gets his name) descended into the depths, gone behind the sea to bring light to the underworld and gone to the *Untergang*.[165] This "go(ing) down" (*untergehen*) and "down-going" (*Untergang*) for Nietzsche's hermeneutics is the descending of Zarathushtra from the solitude of the mountains into the world of men. Nietzsche's Zarathustra descends below to search for the rightful men.

Now it is said that both *untergehen* and *Untergang* have three meanings: 1) to descend, 2) to set as the sun, and 3) to be destroyed. They are anti-thesis to the term *Aufhebung* which itself has three combined meanings: 1) to lift up, 2) to preserve, and 3) abolish. *Aufhebung* is the "lifting up" of reality at a higher level of existence in direct contrast to *Untergang* which implies a state of ruins. But why has Zarathushtra gone to the realm of this "down below": the *Untergang* of Nietzsche, or the land of the demonical *devas* and the abnormal heat?

According to Iranian legend, the world of people is not the world of the underworld. The underworld is the world of evil, probably the world inhabited not only by those who worship the mischief demons (*devas*), but the demons themselves. Everything "down below" is evil—the realm of *Ahriman*.

In Iranian legend, Yima also known as Jamshid (if not the founder of world civilization, then at least the Iranian one) apparently sins and is literally driven (or forced) into the underworld. The *Vevdidâd* mentions how a wicked winter causes the snow to melt creating terrible floods. Jamshid builds an enclosure (*Var*) to escape the flood wherein he retreats with the seeds of all healthy people, animals, and trees, even eatables.[166] Now Jamshid besides being the great hero of the Iranian world—he not only founds civilization, but also discovers the production of weapons, the weaving of textiles, the consanguine marriage system and class society[167]—is also a sinner. Now the nature of his sin is not very clear, though a Marxist reading would say that he produced class society and thus he erred, while a Freudian reading would suggest that his sin was due to the institutionalization of incest. Nineteenth and early twentieth century renderings of Zarathushtra's *Gathas*, on the contrary, said that Jamshid slaughtered the good ox (or cow) to achieve immortality, but achieved only the opposite result.[168] Jamshid (the Iranian hero) is some sort of an Iranian Faust. It is said that he flirted with a demon and was temporarily possessed, but the female demon was exorcised, Jamshid then reformed, and went back to his people, teaching them the next-to-kin marriage,[169] which even today, the modern Zoroastrians are supposed to practise. Elsewhere it is said (that like Faust) he chases Ahriman (the devil) and even puts his hands in the devil's buttocks to extract *Paymān* or "the correct measure"—implying that to be good (again a Faustian theme) one has to flirt with evil.[170] The last explanation is that Jamshid was actually an atheist, and when Ahura Mazda tried making a covenant with him, he refused. But whatever it may be—Jamshid, the hero, remains a sinner, in fact the first sinner, and in some ways, the first definite mortal—because *Ahura Mazda's* gift to humanity, immortality, is lost because of the first sin. But this sin will not affect only Jamshid. It also affects his people. They, or at least their memory, goes below—into the region of the repressed unconscious.

Now Zarathushtra himself mentions Jamshid, claiming that he will not do what Jamshid did.[171] Again it is not very clear from Zarathushtra himself what Jamshid did. But Zarathushtra is not Jamshid. Jamshid is a king, in fact the first king, but Zarathushtra is far above kingship. Zarathustra is the chosen one of Ahura Mazda. Then why did Zarathushtra have to go underground, post-651 C.E.? And why did Zarathushtra's prediction that the New Messiah would come turn out to be devastating for his followers?

Zarathushtra is thus no longer the one who heralds the Golden Dawn, or if he is, then he heralds it in the underworld. According to Nietzsche his descent into the underworld is because of the uncanny state of human existence.[172] As is well known, for at least those acquainted with psychoanalysis, the uncanny (*das Unheimlich*) is a state of a mental disorder which induces a feeling of unhomeliness (as the term *Unheimlich* suggests) as well as the arousal of the feeling of terror and the desire for the death-wish.[173] For Zarathushtra, the uncanny state of the "down below" is hell (*Drujō Demānē*), literally "the abode of untruth,"[174] and "the domain of the worst mind" (*Acištahyā demānē Manahō*).[175]

But why has the founder of Utopia gone underground? Why do people in his own land either not know him or actively repress him? What does Zarathushtra in the underworld mean? The underworld is not only the region of the demons and *Ahriman*. It is also the region of denial. To deny one's freedom is to go underground. It is to give consent to this politics of the repressed unconscious. Now his followers who reside in India do not follow this thread of thought. Rather it is the secular forces in Iran who raise the question: Why does theology in contrast to the freedom that the ancient Persians taught become the ideology-in-dominance in Iran? And why is human freedom denied for the politics of an inverted Utopia even today?

For certain secular forces in Iran who need to reinvent a pre-Islamic past in order for freedom to reign in Iran, one must recall the Hegelian dictum: *one cannot go back into history*. But all secular forces in Iran are clear—the violent political-theology of the theocratic elite and the nexus between the mullahs and the state cannot remain for long. One needs, we hear, not sermons of the clerics, but Kant, Marx, Habermas, Rawls and Derrida. There are other voices that one hears that say that the cosmopolitan traditions of Iran are based on Cyrus the Great and not on the politics of superstition, medievalism, economic backwardness and persecution. Other voices claim that for an authentic libertarian tradition one needs to retrieve Zarathushtra from the underworld of active forgetfulness. Zarathushtra they say is not only for some few hundred thousand people. Zarathushtra, the thinker of human freedom, they say, has to return to Iran. If the sun has set on the land of this thinker, then this night of darkness will necessarily be over. One cannot stop dreaming of Utopia. In this Romantic remembrance one recalls Hegel's reading of Zarathushtra:

> The terrestrial world is the seat and the ground of the battle between good and evil; but the battle between light and darkness is not an absolutely and inherently unresolved opposition, but a transient one. Ohrmuzd, the principle of light will conquer.[176]

Parsis, Colonialism and Modernity

In the understanding of how a minority assumes a position of hegemony and the vanguard of social change, one has to insist that one cannot refer to essentialist explanations. On the other hand, one has to grasp the logic of secularization and modernity in India with the Parsis at its forefront. If Max Weber had said that one needed in Europe a "spirit of capitalism" and it would not be served by the feudal catholic ideology that had become (to borrow Engels's phrase) "an international centre of feudalism,"[177] but Protestantism that needed to infuse the spirit of capitalism; so too in India one needed this self-same spirit of entrepreneurship. The Parsis were prepared to wear the hat of the bourgeoisie. For that, however, the crowns of the pre-capitalist feudal lords had to be knocked off. And for that the old orthodox ideas too had to be obliterated, and obliteration that was brought about by English education. According to Dadabhai Naoroji:

> This difference (between the orthodox and the liberals) is so wide and marked, that in describing the present condition and customs of the Parsis, statements about one portion will sometimes be altogether inapplicable to another.....It is not the usual difference in the domestic habits of a people, arising from differences of means, occupation, society, etc. but a revolution caused in one portion by external causes the influences of English education and example.[178]

Historians have quite often argued as to how the Parsis, even though numerically always very small, could influence the course of modern Indian history. There are differing explanations. According to Daniel Buchanan, the Parsis were "racially" and "culturally" distinct from other Indian communities which was "agreeable to European taste,"[179] thus allowing them to form a part of the elite in British India, while Robert Kennedy mentions the "world affirming" attitude of the Parsis along with the emphasis on labour.[180] Both are not off the mark. Yet sociological explanations miss out the deep structures embedded within Persian culture with its accumulation of class contradictions reflected in the ideological superstructure which the Parsis carry even today. Quite often it is said that it is their prophet's words: "good thoughts, good words and good deeds" which form the contours of their repertoire. I would disagree slightly and claim that it is the accumulation of contradictions embodied in the Persian heritage which on the one hand has the spirit of the Persian Empire and on the other hand the politics of Iranian communism.[181] This contradictory spirit is largely unnoticed. What one finds instead the praxis oriented nature of the Parsi ideologists which can best be grasped in Dadabhoi Naoroji's words:

> We must go on doing our duty, and nature will work out its own result. We have to put nature into motion. If we don't do so, nature by its inertia will remain still.[182]

One important point that needs to be stressed is that since the Parsis reappear on the stage of history with the coming of capitalism in India, they appear dressed as the colonial elite. According to the anthropologist Luhrmann:

> Indeed, all of the virtues reconfigured and acquired during the Raj—the honesty of commercial trustworthiness, the purity associated with European-like racial superiority to the native Hindus, the philanthropy of successful business, the English style rationality and the progressiveness of Parsi religion, life-style, educational aims, and even the status of their women—all of these construct a semiotic package of the Parsi as an English gentleman.[183]

There is another view that relates the rise of the Parsis in India and the growth of colonial power. According to this view:

> The incorporation of the Parsis into the economic and political world of British power, from the late eighteenth century, evinced the successful transformation the Parsis effected from minority community in the provincial setting to influential elite in the new urban setting of Bombay. The Parsis' cooperation with the British was based on a keen appreciation of the new environment of opportunity the British were affecting in Western India, on the part of the individual Parsis directly in contact with the British and the part of the community as a whole. Active and voluntary assimilation to British values, furthermore, was based on the personal affinity the Parsi developed in contact with things British. A set of semiotics was adopted by the Parsis in support of the affinity between things British and Parsi, and in praise of Parsi identity under colonial rule. At the same time, the assimilation to British values both completed and functioned alongside the Parsis' commitment to traditional identity.[184]

Probably all serious studies (with the exception of the German sociologist Eckehard Kulke) are based on this thesis of the Parsis and the British Raj. While it is evident that the rise of the Parsi bourgeoisie and the development of colonial capitalism coincided, the colonial narrative seems to miss out three central points—(1) the high Persian heritage of the Parsis which propelled them as the agents of the capitalist mode of production in India, (2) the Parsi apathy for the idyllic Indian village system and the politics of underdevelopment, and (3) the transition from feudalism to capitalism in India and the role of the Parsis in this transition. To come to the point, one will have to recall Marx: "England has to fulfil a double mission in India; one destructive, the other regenerating—the annihilation of old Asiatic society, and the laying of the material foundations of Western society in Asia."[185] One of the missionaries of modernity in India would be the Parsis carrying out at least part of Marx's "double mission".

Instead of the equation: Parsis and the British Raj, it is better to postulate the equation: Parsis (or rather the Parsi bourgeoisie, one must note the Parsi underclass—Herbert Marcuse's "Great Refusal"—has never been represented) and the advent of capitalism in India. When Luhrmann states the views of the contemporary Parsis who seem disenchanted with India, it is class politics which ought to be recorded, rather than the speech-act of an ethnic community. Luhrmann notes how D.F. Karaka dedicated his volume on the Parsis to the Prince of Wales.[186] But Luhrmann also notes the exact opposite of the pro-British image of the Parsis:

> Today (the Parsis) are facing another crisis, and it is largely of their own making. This comes from the almost wholesale imitation of the manners of the West....The relatively much higher standard of life which the Parsis have adopted for themselves....has brought many social and moral evils in its train and has proved disastrous for the well being of the community.[187]

There are two problems that one must note with the theorization on the Parsis—the refusal to theorize on the Parsi proletariat (not to forget Parsi women) and the blinding to the idea of the Parsis living in "Indian feudalism". It is not the case that the Parsis were literally unknown in pre-colonial India. A nineteenth century work on the Parsis, D.F. Karaka's *History of the Parsis*[188] claims that this community were known only from the times of the Achaemenians to the Sasanians and then again with the coming of the British in India, as if from the time of the arrival in India till the coming of the British—i.e. in the age of an alleged "Indian feudalism"—they were almost an unknown people. Presently they are known as one of the pioneers of modernity as also one of the founders of liberalism in not only modern India, but also in large parts of South Asia.

Conclusion

One now closes this little book with a quote from Badiou. According to him:

> No life, no natural power, can be beyond Good and Evil. We should say, rather, that every life, including that of the human animal, is *beneath* Good and Evil.[189]

In consequence of going *beneath* Good and Evil that one recognizes the human condition, that one poses the question: "What is humanity and where are we going?" That there are no essences in the world except the human and natural essence is something that has been spelt out. That Zarathushtra also theorized on this human and natural essence could have quite possibly made him the first theoretician of this human and natural essence. His *messianic historicism* was thus the messianism of the human essence. To search for this human essence is thus natural and has to be the project that one can borrow from Samir Amin's idea of the three waves of universal humanism. The three waves should have a dialogue with one another. Dialogical discourses are the dialogues between all forms of humanisms that are bridges connecting all cultures and civilizations. That humanism starts with a laugh and also ends with one, ought to be a logical conclusion of the humanist enterprise. What clearly stands out is the legendary first laughter of Zarathushtra and his message: seek wisdom (*Mazda*) with the good mind (*Vohu Manah*).

But when Theodor Adorno had once said that: "To write poetry after Auschwitz is barbarism,"[190] then one may now say: "To laugh in the times of imperialism is equally barbaric." Walter Benjamin's document of culture which is simultaneously a document of barbarism reappears on the scene of world history. Just as the philosopher (Aristotle) once marched (even metaphorically) with his barbarian student (Alexander), so too now one sees the march-past of late capitalist ideology with imperialist invasion. One must have, what Adorno said, to have a habit of thinking with one's ears.[191] For what the good mind sees and hears is not so much wisdom, but the march past of Ahriman now appearing as the return of the accursed from across the Western borders, who, like Alexander the father of Western imperialism, is now knocking not only at the doors of Iran, but on all the doors of each and every nation of the world. But what one has probably not realized is that just as Alexander did not stop with Iran, so too the New Alexander is not going to stop its barbaric raids there. For when he is knocking at the doors of Iran he is also simultaneously knocking at the doors of India. One may just have to stop laughing. And since the messiah is yet missing and has not yet descended either as the Zoroastrian Saviour or the Shiite Imam, to save both Iran and the world at large, one will have to hear and think aloud with the ears, not of the transcendental World Saviours who are perpetually missing, but of collective humanity so as to hear the lament of both the bard and the revolutionary:

Should this torture then torment us
Since it brings us greater pleasure?
Were not through the rule of Timur
Souls devoured without measure?[192]

NOTES

1. Walter Benjamin, 'Eduard Fuchs. Collector and Historian', in *One-Way Street and Other Writings*, trans. Edmund Jephocott and Kingsley Shorter (London: New Left Books, 1979), p. 359.
2. Note that in Nietzsche the "h" in Zarathushtra is missing. Zarathushtra becomes Zarathustra.
3. G.W.F. Hegel, *The Philosophy of History*, trans. J. Sibree (New York: Prometheus Books, 1991), p. 4.
4. Ibid., p. 173.
5. See Mary Boyce and Franz Grenet, *History of Zoroastrianism, Vol. Three, Under. Macedonian and Roman Rule* (Leiden: E.J. Brill, 1991), pp. 368, 523.
6. For understanding Zoroastrianism and the origins of monotheism see Mary Boyce's *Zoroastrianism: A Shadowy but Powerful Presence in the Judeo-Christian World* (London: Dr. William's Trust, 1987) which is a study on the influence of Zoroastrian thought on the formation of Judaism and Christianity. Also see Mary Boyce, *Zoroastrians. Their Religious Beliefs and Practices* (London: Routledge, 1979) and Mary Boyce, *History of Zoroastrianism, Volume Two, Under the Achaemenians* (Leiden: E.J. Brill, 1982); Mary Boyce and Franz Grenet, *History of Zoroastrianism, Volume Three, Under Macedonian and Roman Rule.*
7. Anaximander of Miletus (c. 610-546 B.C.E.), Thales of Miletus (c. 624-547 B.C.E.), Anaximenes of Miletus (c. 588-525 B.C.E.), Heraclitus of Ephesus (c 544-483 B.C.E.) and Pythagoras of Samos (c. 580-500 B.C.E.] all echo Zoroastrian cosmology. See Mary Boyce, *History of Zoroastrianism. Under the Achaemaenians, Vol. Two,* pp. 47, 150-163 who mentions the origins of Greek philosophy in Iran.
8. According to classical Zoroastrian sources as stated in the *Kisseh-e-Sanjan,* the date of the arrival is 785 C.E. This text says that after the collapse of the Sasanians, a group of Zoroastrians fled to Kohistan (a mountains range in Iran) and dwelled there for a hundred years. After that they went to Hormuz in the Persian Gulf where they stayed for fifteen years and then sailed in seven ships to India. They landed in Div where they stayed for nineteen years and then moved to Sanjan where, as Parsi legend claims, they met Jadi Rana who after the symbolic exchange of sugar and milk gave them refuge. See Jivanji Modi, *A Few*

Events in the Early History of the Parsis and their Dates (Mumbai: K.R. Cama Oriental Institute, 2004), p. 9. For the tenth century dating see John Hinnells 'The Modern Zoroastrian Diaspora', in J.M. Brown and R. Foot (ed.), *Migration: The Asian Experience* (Macmillan, 1994), p. 56, Mary Boyce, *The Textual Sources for the Study of Religion* (Manchester: Manchester University Press, 1984), p. 24.

9. R.C. Zaehner, *The Dawn and Twilight of Zoroastrianism* (London: Weidenfeld and Nicholson, 1961). But the modern Parsis living in India, which has the largest population, followed by their brethren in Iran, Pakistan, Western Europe, North America, Australia and New Zealand, do not consider themselves as exilic people or as if living in the twilight of their history.
10. The legend of Zarathushtra's first laugh at the time of his birth which Pliny mentioned is stated in the *Dînkard*, Book VII.
11. 'Selections from the *Zâd-Sparam', in Pahlavi Texts. Part V. Marvels of Zoroastrianism*, trans. E.W. West (Delhi: Motilal Banarasdas, 1965), p. 149.
12. Ibid.
13. Ibid., p. 150.
14. See Aturpāt-I Ēmētān, *The Wisdom of the Sasanian Sages. Dînkard VI*, trans Shaul Shaked (Colorodo: Westview Press, 1979), p. 11.
15. See Helmut Humbach, *The Gāthās of Zarathushtra and Other Old Avestan Texts* in collaboration with Josef Elfenbein and Prods O. Skjaervo Part I (Heidelberg: Carl Winter Universitätsverlag, 1991), pp. 24-5.
16. Ibid., p. 25.
17. See *Pahlavi Vendidâd (Zand=Î Jvît-Dêv=Dât)*, transliteration and translation by B.T. Anklesaria (Mumbai: K.R. Cama Oriental Institute, 2002), p. 3.
18. Ibid., pp. 15-38.
19. Mary Boyce, *Zoroastrianism. Its Antiquity and Constant Vigour* (New York: Mazda Publishers, 1992), p. 32.
20. 'The Gathas of Zarathushtra', trans I.J.S. Taraporewalla in *The Religion of Zarathushtra* (Bombay: B.I. Taraporewalla 1979), Y. 29.1, p. 104; Y. 29.9, p. 112.
21. Ibid., Y. 32.3, p. 150.
22. Ibid., Y. 46.1, p. 240.
23. Ibid., Y. 46.2, p. 241.

24. Due to the erroneous dating of Zarathushtra around the time of Darius's rule, it was inferred that Cyrus was pre-Zarathushtra. The Middle Persian text *Ardā Wirāz Nāmag*, trans. Fereydun Vahman (London: Curzon Press, 1986), p. 191 also follows this false dating which emerges from Sasanian incorrect dating of the prophet. This is clearly incorrect. The political and economic landscape that the *Gathas* indicate are different from Achaemenian times. Mary Boyce, in *History of Zoroastrianism. Under the Achmaenians, Vol. Two,* pp. 43, 47, 212, 216, 222, mentions Cyrus as Zoroastrian as also in *Zoroastrianism. Its Antiquity and Constant Vigour*, p. 28..
25. See Gherardo Gnoli, *Zoroaster's Time and Homeland. A Study on the Origins of Mazdeism and Related Problems* (Naples, 1980), p. 215.
26. 'The Gathas of Zarathushtra', trans I.J.S. Taraporewalla, Y. 46.2, p. 241.
27. The Greco mentioning of Zarathushtra writing with gold ink is probably more speculative than real.
28. R.C. Zaehner, *The Dawn and Twilight of Zoroastrianism*, p. 25.
29. Mary Boyce, *Textual Sources for the Study of Religion* (Manchester: Manchester University Press, 1984), p. 23.
30. See Richard Frye, 'Zoroastrianism in Central Asia before Islam', in *A Zoroastrian Tapestry. Art, Religion and Culture,* ed. Pheroza J. Godrej and Firoza Punthakey Mistree (Ahmedabad: Mapin Publishers, 2002); Frantz Grenet, 'Zoroastrian Themes on Early Medieval Sogdian Ossuaries', in Ibid., pp. 91-97.
31. 'The Gospel according to Mathew', in *The Holy Bible* (New York: Wm. Collins, 1946), p. 1.
32. Mary Boyce in *The History of Zoroastrianism, Vol. Three* mentions how the Christian legend of resurrection has distinct echoes of Zoroastrian eschatology where the soul of the departed stays on the earth for three days and then proceeds on its celestial journey.
33. 'The Gathas of Zarathushtra', Y. 30.3, p. 117. Also Y. 30.4, p. 118; Y 30.5, p. 119.
34. Ibid, Y. 30.3, p. 117.
35. Ibid.
36. Ibid.
37. Ibid., Y. 30.4, p. 118.

38. Martin Haug, *The Paris. Essays on their Sacred Language, Writings and Religion* (New Delhi: Cosmos Publications, 1978), p. 303.
39. 'The Gathas of Zarathushtra', Y. 30.3, p. 117.
40. *Zand-Ākāsīh. Iranian or Greater Bundahišn*, transliteration and translated by B.T. Anklesaria (Bombay: Rahnumae Mazdaysnan Sabha, 1956), 'Traditional Information, [Genesis]', p. 3.
41. What seems to be a Zoroastrian-Islam conflict in Iranian history was in actuality a conflict that emerged between the national-popular masses: the peasant against landed property and the nobility. The political economy of the history of class struggles that governed the collapse of Zoroastrianism has yet to be written.
42. *Zand-Ākāsīh. Iranian or Greater Bundahišn*, Chapter XXXIII, 15, p. 277.
43. Richard Frye, *The Heritage of Persia* (London: Weidenfeld and Nicholson, 1975), p. 289, n. 9.
44. Edward Said's *Orientalism* which is a definite critique of the Eurocentric theories of history, however does not suffice, since it does not consider the history of West Asia prior to the middle of the seventh century. The tragedy of Iranian history is that despite Firdausi, Khayaam, Rumi, Nizami, and Sa'di, more is remembered and written on kings and priests, than on the subaltern masses.
45. See Richard Frye, *The Golden Age of Persia. The Arabs in the East* (London: Weidenfeld and Nicholson, 1975), p. 1.
46. Herodotus, *The Persian Wars*, trans. George Rawlinson (New York: The Modern Library, 1942), p. 76.
47. Mary Boyce, 'The Continuity of the Zoroastrian Quest', in *Man's Religious Quest*, ed. Whitfield Foy (London: Croom Helm, 1978).
48. Richard Frye in *The Golden Age of Persia* talks of this continuity of Iran despite the changes in economies, political dynasties and religions.
49. *Zand-Ākāsīh. Iranian or Greater Bundahišn*, Chapter XXXIII, 35, p. 283.
50. In ancient Iran the genealogy of the king-prophet-hero starts with the first man, Gayômart, a role that Jamshid tragically refuses. But unlike Jamshid who refuses to wear the glory of the prophet, Zarathushtra takes on the role conferred onto him and becomes the prophet par excellence

51. In 1979 Ayatollah Khomeni became this king-quasi-prophet—the legendary Missing Imam who had descended on earth.
52. 'Selections from the *Zâd-Sparam*', pp. 150, 152-3.
53. See Ehsan Yarshater, 'Mazdakism' in *The Cambridge History of Iran, Vol. 3, (2). The Selucids, Parthians and the Sasanian Periods* (Cambridge: Cambridge University Press, 1986), p. 991. It would be interesting to note whether the Mazdakites still exist even if they externally appear to conform to mainstream Islam.
54. Firdausi, *Shâhnâma,* Vol. VII, trans. Arthur George Warner and Edmund Warner (London: Kegan Paul, 1915), p. 205.
55. See Ehsan Yarshater, 'Mazdakism', p. 997.
56. Ibid. See also *Vendidâd*, p. 87.
57. Ibid.
58. Firdausi, op. cit., pp. 207-8.
59. Ibid., p. 208.
60. Ibid., p. 204.
61. Quoted in Ehsan Yarshater, 'Mazdakism', p. 998.
62. R.C. Zaehner, *Zurvan. A Zoroastrian Dilemma* (Oxford: The Clarendon Press, 1955), p. 9.
63. R.C. Zaehner in *The Dawn and Twilight of Zoroastrianism,* p. 217, says that the *Gayômarteans* were sects of the pre-Zarathushtra Magis of Iran.
64. See Ibid., pp. 186, 188, 192, 196-7, 198-203, 246.
65. Ibid., pp. 180-1.
66. Ibid., p. 171.
67. Ibid.
68. Karl Marx, *Notes on Indian History (664-1858)* (Moscow: Progress Publishers, 1947), pp. 13-4.
69. Ibid., p. 13.
70. See *The Letter of Tansar,* trans. Mary Boyce (Roma: Instituto Italino Per Il Medo Edestremo Oriente, 1968). The irony is that even the right-wing mullah movement in contemporary Iran has clear echoes which can be found in Sasanian Iran.
71. *Ahd Ardašīr*, ed. I. Abbas, Beirut, 1967. See also *The Letter of Tansar*, trans. Mary Boyce and the fourth volume of the encyclopaedic *Dînkard* which narrates the history of the identity of religion and the state in Zoroastrian Iran. Also see 'The Instruments of

Religion', in Shaul Shaked, *Dualism in Transformation. Varieties of Religion in Sasanian Iran* (London: School of Oriental and African Studies, 1994), pp. 99-131.

72. See 'Mihr Nyaish', in *The Nyaishes or Zoroastrian Litanies*, ed. and trans. M.N. Dhalla (New York: AMS Press Inc., 1965), p. 66, *Ardā Wirazf Nāmag*, trans Fereydun Vahman (London: Curzon Press, 1986), p. 77.

73. One motif is clearly seen: Was this handing of the *Avesta* to Aristotle the culmination of the Greek borrowing from Iran, which began with Aleximander and Heraclitus and then perfected by Plato? After all the Heraclitean theme: "everything is in a flux" is Zarathushtra's invention and Plato's "Idea" (in fact the entire "Logos" and "Nous" of Greek philosophy) is said to be a direct borrowing from the Zoroastrian "*Fravashi*", or "the Transcendental Essence". Likewise the Platonic doctrine of the philosopher-king is also probably nothing but the transcription of the real politics of the Persian monarch Cyrus the Great. Explicitly this theme of Iranian borrowings by the Greeks was probably first recognized in the middle of the nineteenth century by the German philologist Martin Haug and then a little later by Richard Reitzenstein. But besides these two thinkers it was the infant terrible of German philosophy Friedrich Nietzsche who in his *Also sprach Zarathustra* immortalized the name of Zarathushtra. Following Nietzsche it is Zarathushtra who teaches the will to life, as against the will to death. And for Nietzsche Western Reason that is built on the reactive force—from Socrates via Pauline Christianity to Schopenhauer—is hurling to its own demise.

74. 'Chronicles', pp. 410-1, 'The Book of Ezra', pp. 411-6, 'The Book of Isaiah', p. 640, in *The Holy Bible* (New York: Wm. Collins, 1946). 'The Gospel According to Mathew', in *The Holy Bible*, p. 1.

75. Friedrich Nietzsche, *Thus Spoke Zarathustra* (London: Penguin, 1983), p. 39.

76. Ibid.

77. *Zand-Ākāsīh. Iranian or Greater Bundahišn*, Chapter XXXIII, 35, p. 279.

78. See Christopher Buck, 'Bahá'u'lláh as Zoroastrian Saviour', in *Baha'i Studies Review*, Vol. 8 (1998).

79. J. Gerson Da Cunha, *The Origin of Bombay* (Chennai: Asian Educational Services, 2004), p. 314.

80. See Susan Stiles Maneck, *The Death of Ahriman: Culture, Identity and Theological Change Among the Parsis of India* (Bombay: K.R. Cama Oriental Institute, 1997), p. 44, n. 2.
81. See Ehsan Yarshater, 'Mazdakism' in *The Cambridge History of Iran, Vol. 3, (2). The Selucids, Parthians and the Sasanian Periods* (Cambridge: Cambridge University Press, 1986), p. 1004.
82. Mary Boyce, 'Middle Persian Literature', in *Handbuch der Orientalistik, Erste Abteilung. Der Nahe und der Mittlere Osten* (London: Brill, 1968), p. 32.
83. Richard Frye, *The Golden Age of Persia*, pp. 7-26.
84. See Richard Frye, *The Heritage of Persia* (London: Weidenfeld and Nicholson, 1962), p. 235.
85. Ibid., p. 239.
86. Ibid., pp. 234-55.
87. *Pahlavi Vendidâd*, p. 259. "*I*-drive-away (the dêv) Indra; *I*-drive-away (*the* dêv) Saurva; *I*-drive-away Naonhaithya-dêv from *the*-house, from *the*-street, from *the*-village, from *the*-country."
88. Ibid., pp. 12-13.
89. Karl Marx, 'The British Rule in India', in *Marx. Engels. On Colonialism* (Moscow: Progress Publishers, 1976), p. 40.
90. See Susan Stiles Maneck, op. cit., p. 53.
91. J. Duchesne-Guillemin, *Religion of Iran* (Bombay: Tata Press, 1973), p. 259.
92. Ahura Mazda is essentially good—this is the bedrock of Zoroastrianism. Ahura Mazda is not, as R.C. Zaehner informs us in *The Teachings of the Magis* like the Biblical Yahweh who creates Adam and Eve and then vents fury because Eve dared to disobey God. This idea of God getting angry is probably a synthesis of two Jewish traditions—where the first idea of a good, omnipotent God is meshed up with the second rendering where the exilic Jews bring their tribal pagan god (the volcanic god) who is continuously erupting.
93. Yet Ahura Mazda is different from the Judaic God Yahweh in the sense that Ahura Mazda does not drive all other godly beings away, in order to reign supreme. Neither is Ahura Mazda a purely transcendent Being (like Parmeneides's "Being") totally distinct from the material world. In Zoroastrianism the "Ideal" and the "Material", the "One" and the "Many" are always

dialectically related. Ahura Mazda permeates all existence and presents itself in a pantheistic way.

94. Friedrich Nietzsche, *Ecce Homo* (London: Penguin, 1992), p. 127.
95. Johann Wolfgang Von Goethe, *Faust*, Part One, trans. Philip Wayne (London: Penguin, 1949), p. 67
96. Substance, attribute and mode from Spinoza's *Ethics*, trans. Andrew Boyle (London: Everyman, 1993), p. 3.
97. G.W.F. Hegel, *Science of Logic*, trans. A.V. Miller (London: George Allen & Unwin, 169), p. 82; G.W.F. Hegel, *Wissenschaft der Logik* (Frankfurt am Main: Suhrkamp Verlag, 1983), p. 83.
98. "Lack" is borrowed from the philosophy of Ludwig Feuerbach's *The Essence of Christianity*, trans. George Elliot (London: Harper & Row, 1957).
99. 'The Gathas of Zarathushtra', in trans. I.J.S. Taraporewalla, in *The Religion of Zarathushtra* (Bombay: B.I. Taraporewalla, 1979), Y. 30.3, p. 117.
100. Ibid.
101. Ibid.
102. Ibid., Y. 30.3, p. 116.
103. Ibid.
104. Ibid., Y. 30.1, p. 115.
105. The theme of Zoroastrianism as "dualist" has a long history probably starting with the first Christian writers in Sasanian times. But it was the not so reverend Reverend John Wilson who in the middle of the nineteenth century criticized Zoroastrianism as dualism suggesting that the devil was equal to the Zoroastrian God. Unwittingly academic Zoroastrianism especially from England picked up this colonial theme. Thus R.C. Zaehner and Mary Boyce are two exponents on the theme of Zoroastrian dualism. In fact, Boyce then concludes from this false claim that Ahura Mazda is not omnipotent. Her alleged Zoroastrian 'students' in India under the rubric of "Zoroastrian Studies" are also proponents of a half-potent Ahura Mazda. For an excellent rendering of Zoroastrian dualism see Shaul Shaked, *Dualism in Transformation. Varieties of Religion in Sasanian Iran* (London: School of Oriental and African Studies, 1994). Helmut Humbach is the latest of the proponents of dualism. He says that Zoroastrianism is "a dualist religion par excellence" in *The Heritage of the Zarathushtra. A New Translation of the Gathas* (Heidelberg: Universitätsverlag C. Winter, 1994), p. 12.

106. G.W.F. Hegel, *Introduction to the Lectures on the History of Philosophy*, trans. T.M. Knox and A.V. Miller (Oxford: Clarendon Press, 1985), pp. 152-3.
107. Friedrich Nietzsche, *Ecce Homo*, trans. R.J. Hollingdale (London: Penguin, 1983), pp. 127-8.
108. Edward Said, 'Orientalism 25 Years Later. Worldly Humanism v. the Empire-Builders', in *Counterpunch*, August 5, 2003.
109. John R. Hinnells, *The Zoroastrian Diaspora. Religion and Migration* (Oxford: Oxford University Press, 2005), p. 709.
110. Philip Kreyenbroek, 'Modern Sects with Ancient Roots. The Yezidis and the Ahl-e Haqq of Kurdistan', in *A Zoroastrian Tapestry. Art, Religion & Culture*, ed. Pheroza J. Godrej and Firoza Punthakey Mistree (Ahmedabad: Mapin Publishing Pvt. Ltd., 2002), pp. 260-77.
111. John Hinnells, op. cit., p. 9
112. Quoted in John R. Hinnells, *The Zoroastrian Diaspora. Religion and Migration* (Oxford: Oxford University Press, 2005), p. 224.
113. John R. Hinnells, op. cit., p. 226.
114. Ibid., p. 227.
115. When I said that the idea of the Parsi is sublated into the practice of citizenship, I will use the Hegelian term *Aufhebung* in order to understand the term sublation (sometimes also translated as supersession and transcendence). Thus what I mean is that this logic of sublation (*Aufhebung*) "lifts up" social identities at a higher level, thus preserving as well as abolishing them, both at the same time. But why, so one may ask: does this Hegelian logic work amongst the Parsis? The answer is simple—the Parsi faith is itself dialectical. Remember that Hegel had said that the prophet of the Parsi faith was the first dialectician in world history. See G.W.F. Hegel, *Introduction to the Lectures on the History of Philosophy*, trans. T.M. Knox and A.V. Miller (Oxford: Clarendon Press, 1985), p. 153.
116. Walter Benjamin, 'Theses on the Philosophy of History', in *Illuminations*, trans. Harry Zohn (Glasgow: Fontana/Collins, 1979), pp. 263-4; 'Eduard Fuchs, Collector and Historian', in *One Way Street*, trans. Edmund Jephocott and Kingsley Shorter (London: New Left Books, 1979), p. 352.
117. Abbas Milani, 'Zoroaster and the Ayatollahs', in *The National Interest*, January-February, 2011.

118. R.C. Zaehner, op. cit., p. 19.
119. 'The Kisseh-e-Sanjan', in Shapurshah Hormasji Hodivala (ed.) *Studies in Parsi History* (Bombay, 1920), p. 98.
120. Karl Marx and Frederick Engels, *The German Ideology* (Moscow: Progress Publishers, 1976), p. 101.
121. Ibid.
122. *Azerbaijan Prose. An Anthology*, ed. Mirza Ibragminov (Moscow: Progress Publishers, 1977), p. 14.
123. Ibid., p. 5.
124. Ibid.
125. 'The Gathas of Zarathushtra', Y. 30.7, p. 121.
126. Karl Marx and Frederick Engels, 'Manifesto of the Communist Party', in *Marx. Engels. Selected Works* (Moscow: Progress Publishers, 1975), p. 35; 'Manifest der kommunistischen Partei', in *Karl Marx. Die Frühschriften* (Stuttgart: Dietz Verlag, 1964), p. 525.
127. Abbas Milani, op. cit.
128. Walter Benjamin, 'Theses on the Philosophy of History', in *Illuminations*, trans. Harry Zohn (Glasgow: Fontana/Collins, 1979), pp. 259-60.
129. *Ahid Ardašīr*, ed. I. 'Abbas (Beirut, 1967). See Shaul Shaked 'Esoteric Teachings in Zoroastrianism. Appendix D. Secret Religion and Heresy in the Sasanian Theory of Government', in *From Zoroastrian Iran to Islam* (Hampshire: Ashgate Publishing Limited, 1995), pp. 214-9. Josef Wieshofer in his *Ancient Persia. From 550 B.C. to 650 A.D.*, trans. Azizeh Azadi (London: I.B. Tauris Publishers, 2001), p. 211 contradicts the view that the Sasanian state was based on the unity of religion and kingship. For him this mythical identity is the product of later Zoroastrian imagination of the ideal state, maybe even the invention of Muslim writers like al-Mas'udi.
130. Karl Marx, 'The Eighteenth Brumaire of Louis Bonaparte', in *Marx. Engels. Selected Works* (Moscow: Progress Publishers, 1975), pp. 96-7.
131. Samir Amin, *Capitalism in the Age of Globalization . The Management of Contemporary Society* (New Delhi: Madhyam Books, 1997), pp. 80-90.
132. R.C. Zaehner, *The Dawn and Twighlight of Zoroastrianism*, p. 36.

133. Friedrich Nietzsche, *Thus Spoke Zarathustra*, trans. R.J. Hollingdale (London: Penguin, 1983), p. 45.
134. Johann Wolfgang Goethe, *Faust*, Part One, trans. Philip Wayne (London: Penguin, 1949), p. 79.
135. R.C. Zaehner, *The Teachings of the Magis. A Compendium of Zoroastrian Beliefs* (London: George Allen &Unwin, 1956), p. 140.
136. Karl Marx, 'A Contribution to the Critique of Hegel's Philosophy of Right. Introduction', in *Karl Marx. Early Writings*, trans. Rodney Livingstone (New York: Vintage Books, 1975), p. 244.
137. *The Koran*, trans. J.M. Rodwell (London: Everyman, 1983), Sura X. 48, p. 279, Sura XIV. 4, p. 226, Sura XV. 38, p. 202.
138. Frederick Engels, 'To Karl Marx in London, June 6, 1853', in *Marx. Engels. Selected Correspondence* (Moscow: Progress Publishers, 1975) p. 77.
139. Karl Marx 'To Frederick Engels in Manchester, July, 27, 1854', in Ibid., p. 80.
140. Karl Marx, *Capital. A Critique of Political Economy*, trans. Samuel Moore and Edward Aveling (Moscow: Progress Publishers, 1983), p. 703.
141. Frederick Engels, 'To Karl Marx in London. June 6, 1853', in *Marx. Engels. Selected Correspondence*, p. 78.
142. Karl Marx, 'The Future Results of the British Rule in India', in *Marx. Engels. On Colonialism*, p. 82.
143. See Peter Hudis, 'Marx Among the Muslims', in *Capitalism, Nature, Socialism*, December 2004, pp. 53-4.
144. Ibid., p. 53.
145. Pheroza J. Godrej and Firoza Punthakey Mistree, (ed.), *A Zoroastrian Tapestry. Art, Religion & Culture*, (Ahmedabad: Mapin Publishing Pvt. Ltd., 2002).
146. *Zand-Ākāsih. Iranian or Greater Bundahišn*, transliteration and translation by B.T. Anklesaria (Bombay: Rahnumae Mazdayasan Sabha, 1965), p. 127.
147. Friedrich Nietzsche, *Thus Spoke Zarathustra*, p. 97.
148. *Zand-Ākāsīh. Iranian or Greater Bundahišn*, Ch. IV, p. 47.
149. On the Red-Badged or Red-Clothed, see Ehsan Yarshater, 'Mazdakism', in *The Cambridge History of Iran, Vol. 3 (2). The Selucids, Parthain and Sasanian*, ed. Ehsan Yarshater (Cambridge: Cambridge University Press, 1986), pp. 1003-4.

150. *Zand-Ākāsīh. Iranian or Greater Bundahišn,* pp. 277, 279.
151. Ibid., p. 311.
152. *Pahlavi Vendidâd (Zand=Î Jvît-Dêv=Dât),*, 2002), p. 13.
153. 'The Kisseh-e-Sanjan', in Shapurshah Hormasji Hodivala (ed.), p. 102.
154. The process is of course complicated, where cooperation along with conflict operated together, and more often than not, rather than religion playing a dominant role, it was political economy that played a vital role. The shift to the occupying forces and the hegemony of Islam in Iran was because of the ruling classes wanting to continue as the dominant class in Iran. To point to merely one illustration, after the death of the last Sasanian monarch Yazdegird III, part of the elite imperial guard of the king shifted alliance towards the Arabs and fought alongside them. See Richard N. Frye, *The Golden Age of Persia. The Arabs in the East*, pp. 61, 94, who mentions how the *asawira*, or the elite Persian cavalary corps, of the *jund-I shahanshai*, or imperial guard converted to Islam to escape the *jizya* tax, besides intending to be on the winning side and a part of the new ruling elite.
155. *Zand-Ākāsīh. Iranian or Greater Bundahišn,* p. 279.
156. The *Zand-Ākāsīh. Iranian or Greater Bundahišn,* notes how, "orthodoxy has vanished and fled form *the* magnates, and respectability from *the* upholders-of-religion, deep wonderful utterances, and *the* proper reasoning of things……have faded from the memory and knowledge of the populace." Ibid., p. 3.
157. Ibid.
158. Ibid, p. 307.
159. Ibid.
160. Ibid.
161. Friedrich Nietzsche, *Ecce Hommo*, p. 128.
162. Karl Marx, 'The Eighteenth Brumaire of Louis Bonaparte', in *Marx. Engels. Selected Works* (Moscow: Progress Publishers, 1975), p. 96.
163. 'Ethics, Politics and History: An Interview with Jürgen Habermas conducted by Jean-Marie Ferry', in *Universalism vs. Particularism. Contemporary Debates in Ethics*, ed. David Rasmusssen (Cambridge: The MIT Press, 1990), p. 211.
164. Zarathushtra's descent in the underworld is ironically both a Nietzschean theme as well as a real one for the Zoroastrians.

Ironically this theme is carried out in Shiite Islam where the Twelfth Imam literally disappears, and is said to have gone into occultation, and like the Zoroastrian saviour would return again. The theme of the eternal recurrence of the saviour is both a Zoroastrian theme as well as a Shiite one. But in contrast to the Faustian play of good and evil that we have pointed out (both good and evil are said to be rigorously distinct in Zoroastrianism, yet joined together as "twins"); in contemporary political Islam one has the Dostoevskyean theme of: *anything is permissible.* Modern political Islam seems quite similar to the teachings of Bakunin and Georges Sorel. What is produced after the masterpiece in Arabic literary history, the *Koran,* is the politics of rebellion similar to romantic anti-capitalism which echoes Dostoevsky's central question: *Is anything permissible?* After all, one knows that the anarchists with their metaphysics of violence can move any way—either the infantile extreme left-wing way of the nineteenth century *Narodniki* type, or the right shift into the fascist militias. It is in this humanist space that one asks: In the hegemony of the Shiite and Wahabi traditions in Islam, is it actually existing evangelic Christianity and Islam that have failed, or religion per se? If Slavoj Žižek has claimed that one must rescue Christianity from the fundamentalists [Slavoj Žižek, *The Fragile Absolute or, Why is the Christian Legacy Worth Fighting For?* (London: Verso, 2000)], then can one ask the same about Islam? But how would Zarathushtra help? And combined with this critique of anarchism one will also have to look at another site of operation—the Asiatic Mode of Production—the most under-theorized part of the contemporary social sciences—that which makes possible the politics of the authoritarian personality. So how should one humanize the question of religion and how can Zarathushtra the subaltern who went underground speak? Can this subaltern find its voice, the voice of freedom?

165. Friedrich Nietzsche, *Thus Spoke Zarathushtra,* trans. R.J. Hollingdale (London: Penguin, 1983), p. 39.

166. *Pahlavi Vendidâd (Zand=Î Jvît-Dêv=Dât),* pp. 26, 28-30, 35, 37.

167. Shaul Shaked, 'First Man, First King: Notes on Semitic-Iranian Syncretism and Iranian Mythological Transformations', in *From Zoroastrian Iran to Islam* (Hampshire: Ashgate Publishing Limited, 1995), p. 241.

168. See James Moulton, *The Treasure of the Magi* (London: Oxford University Press, 1917, reprinted by The K.R. Cama Oriental

Institute, Mumbai, 2006), p. 31; J. Duchsne-Guillemin, *Religion of Ancient Iran*, trans. K.M. Jamsp Asa (Bombay: Tata Press, 1973), p. 144; Helmut Humbach, *The Gathas of Zarathushtra and Other Old Avestan Texts*, Part I, (Heidelberg, Carl Winter Universitätsverlag, 1991), pp. 57, 133.

169. Shaul Shaked, op. cit.
170. Ibid. Shaked denies this theme as Zoroastrian, as the latter rigorously differentiates good and evil.
171. 'The Gathas of Zarathushtra', trans. I.J.S. Taraporewala, Y. 33.6, p. 169.
172. Friedrich Nietzsche, op. cit., p. 49.
173. Sigmund Freud, 'The Uncanny' in *The Penguin Freud Library*, Vol. 14, *Art and Literature* (London: Penguin, 1985), pp. 339-376.
174. 'The Gathas of Zarathushtra', trans. I.J.S. Taraporewalla, *The Religion of Zarathushtra*, Y. 46.11, p. 250, Y. 51.14, p. 313.
175. Ibid., Y. 32.13, p. 160.
176. G.W.F. Hegel, *Introduction to Lectures on the Philosophy of History*, p. 153.
177. Frederick Engels, 'Socialism: Utopian and Scientific', in *Marx. Engels. Selected Works* (Moscow: Progress Publishers, 1975), p. 383.
178. Dadabhai Naoroji, *The Parsee Religion & the Manners and Customs of the Parsees* (The K.R. Cama Oriental Institute, 2005), p. 50.
179. Daniel Houston Buchanan, *The Development of Capitalistic Enterprise in India*, (New York: Macmillan, 1934), p. 144.
180. Robert E. Kennedy, 'The Protestant Ethic and the Parsis', in *American Journal of Sociology*, No. 68 (1962/63).
181. See C. Tavadia, 'A Pahlavi Text on Communism', in *Modi Memorial Volume* (Bombay, 1930).
182. Dadabhai Naoroji, 'To Hyndman, December 30, 1897'. Quoted in Eckehard Kulke, *The Parsis in India. A Minority as Agent of Social Change* (New Delhi: Vikas Publishing House Pvt. Ltd., 1978), p. 258.
183. T.M. Luhrmann, *The Good Parsi. The Fate of a Colonial Elite in a Postcolonial Society* (Delhi: Oxford University Press, 1996), p. 120.
184. Jesse S. Palsetia, *The Parsis of India. Preservation of Identity in Bombay City* (Leiden: Brill, 2001), p. 28.

185. Karl Marx, 'The Future Results of the British Rule in India', in *Marx. Engels, On Colonialism* (Moscow: Progress Publishers, 1976), p. 82.

186. T.M. Luhrmann, op. cit., p. 97.

187. Ibid., p. 135.

188. D.F. Karaka, *History of the Parsees*, 2 Vols. (London, 1884).

189. Alan Badiou, *Ethics. An Essay on the Understanding of Evil*, trans. Peter Hallward (London: Verso, 2001), p. 59.

190. Theodor Adorno, 'Cultural Criticism and Society', in *Prisms*, trans. Samuel and Shirley Weber (Cambridge: The MIT Press, 1981), p. 34.

191. Ibid., p. 19.

192. Johann Wolfgang Von Goethe, *West-östlicehr Divan. An Suleika*, Karl Marx, 'The British Rule in India,' *Marx. Engels. On Colonialism*, p. 41.